DAILY DOWNLOADS
from Heaven

VOLUME 1

Daily Downloads from Heaven
VOLUME 1

by Meghan Williams

DIVINE PURPOSE PUBLISHING
CELEBRATION, FLORIDA

Copyright © 2019 by Meghan Williams

All rights reserved.

No part of this publication may be reproduced, distributed or transmitted in any form or by any means, including photocopying, recording, or other electronic or mechanical methods, without the prior written permission of the publisher, except in the case of brief quotations embodied in critical reviews and certain other noncommercial uses permitted by copyright law. For permission requests, write to the publisher, addressed "Attention: Permission Request," at the email address below.

DiViNE Purpose Publishing
P.O. Box 471004
Celebration, FL. 34747
www.divinepurposepublishing.com
info@divinepurposepublishing.com

Scripture quotations are taken from the following sources:

The King James Version (KJV) Public Domain. The Voice™. (VOICE) Copyright © 2008 by Ecclesia Bible Society. Used by permission. All rights reserved., *Holy Bible*, New Living Translation (NLT), copyright © 1996, 2004, 2015 by Tyndale House Foundation. Used by permission of Tyndale House Publishers, Inc., Carol Stream, Illinois 60188. All rights reserved., Amplified® Bible (AMP), Copyright © 2015 by The Lockman Foundation Used by permission. www.Lockman.org, Amplified® Bible (AMPC), Copyright © 1954, 1958, 1962, 1964, 1965, 1987 by The Lockman Foundation Used by permission. www.Lockman.org, GOD'S WORD (GW) is a copyrighted work of God's Word to the Nations. Quotations are used by permission. Copyright 1995 by God's Word to the Nations. All rights reserved., The Names of God Bible (without notes) © 2011 by Baker Publishing Group., Name pages, book introductions, Calling God by Name sidebars, and topical prayer guide © 2011 by Ann Spangler. From the Names of God Bible. Used by permission of Baker Publishing Group. Scripture quotations marked (TLB) are taken from The Living Bible copyright © 1971. Used by permission of Tyndale House Publishers, Inc., Carol Stream, Illinois 60188. All rights reserved., New King James Version®. Copyright © 1982 by Thomas Nelson. Used by permission. All rights reserved., ESV® Bible (The Holy Bible, English Standard Version®), copyright © 2001 by Crossway, a publishing ministry of Good

News Publishers. Used by permission. All rights reserved., The Passion Translation® (TPT). Copyright © 2017, 2018 by Passion & Fire Ministries, Inc. Used by permission. All rights reserved. ThePassionTranslation.com., THE HOLY BIBLE, NEW INTERNATIONAL VERSION®, NIV® Copyright © 1973, 1978, 1984, 2011 by Biblica, Inc.® Used by permission. All rights reserved worldwide., THE MESSAGE, copyright © 1993, 2002, 2018 by Eugene H. Peterson. Used by permission of NavPress. All rights reserved. Represented by Tyndale House Publishers, Inc., Jubilee Bible (JUB), copyright © 2000, 2001, 2010, 2013 by Russell M. Stendal. Used by permission of Russell M. Stendal, Bogota, Colombia. All rights reserved., The American Standard Version (ASV) Public Domain., Complete Jewish Bible (CJB) by David H. Stern. Copyright © 1998. All rights reserved. Used by permission of Messianic Jewish Publishers, 6120 Day Long Lane, Clarksville, MD 21029. www.messianicjewish.net., quoted by permission. Quotations designated (NET) are from the NET Bible® copyright ©1996-2016 by Biblical Studies Press, L.L.C. http://netbible.com All rights reserved., Scripture quotations marked CSB have been taken from the Christian Standard Bible®, Copyright © 2017 by Holman Bible Publishers. Used by permission. Christian Standard Bible® and CSB® are federally registered trademarks of Holman Bible Publishers., Darby Translation (DARBY) Public Domain., Tree of Life Version (TLV). © 2015 by the Messianic Jewish Family Bible Society. Used by permission of the Messianic Jewish Family Bible Society.

Library of Congress Control Number: 2019903655

ISBN: 978-1-948812-17-7 (paperback)
ISBN: 978-1-948812-18-4 (hardback)
ISBN: 978-1-948812-19-1 (ePub)
ISBN: 978-1-948812-20-7 (Amazon paperback)

Printed in the United States of America

About the Book

Daily Downloads from Heaven is a collection of brief, Bible-based devotionals to encourage, comfort, and exhort you in your daily life. Each nugget gives you truths to ponder that will challenge you to a stronger, deeper walk of faith and foster a deeper relationship with God.

※ ※ ※

About the Author

Meghan Williams is the founder of Dyed4you Ministries. Her passion is hearing the voice of God and helping others do the same. The fact that she gets to do that with luxurious silks and breathtaking art is just a bonus. She has an MA in Media Communications and a PhD in Information Systems. In her previous careers, she worked both in academia and a corporate environment.

※ ※ ※

Acknowledgements

To my mother, Joanne Otto, for her beautiful example of faith, tireless editing, and steadfast support. I am eternally grateful for the family God chose to place me in.

And to Elisa Eaton, for the beautiful book cover, prayer covering, and hours of prophetic banter. I treasure the amazing friends I've been given.

And finally to June Reinke, for taking the time to pray impartation over a stranger simply because God said to. I'm so grateful for divine connections.

✵ ✵ ✵

Beginning Your Journey

Introduction

Allow me to welcome you on a journey: Daily Downloads from Heaven. Though this journey began as one Papa was taking me on, this is not one intended solely for me, but rather one He intended me to invite you along on as well. Whether or not you are comfortable with or accustomed to hearing the voice of God, one thing I know from experience is that He loves to speak to His children and that if you'll stop to listen, you will hear Him.

When I began getting these daily downloads, hearing the voice of God wasn't a new or revolutionary idea for me because I was blessed to grow up in a household with parents who were always "listening" as they liked to say. The me of my youth was frustrated when I wanted quick responses, but the adult me is forever grateful for the example they set because it established a grid for understanding that hearing God was worthwhile and should be done often and intentionally. That example has served me well.

Though as I look back I can clearly see God's hand guiding me at many points in my life, the first time I remember hearing the voice of God was when I was sitting in church, heartbroken, shortly after an ugly breakup, and I heard God tell me to "call Allen." Spoiler alert: Allen is now my husband of 17 years, and that moment marked the beginning of the core of my spiritual walk. Though the road was often rocky, God has clearly been beside me, and the whispers of His Holy Spirit have increased in quantity and volume.

In 2006 God had me begin dyeing silk, not just flags for use in worship but also scarves to wear. He began giving the silks names, correlating scriptures, meanings for each color, and more. An amazing thing began to happen: testimonies began to come back to me as I gave the silks away, and God blessed this work, which ultimately turned into Dyed4you Ministries. Over the next decade it grew and expanded. I began creating prophetic artwork via Dyed4you Art. Papa brought a team of people alongside to support the ministry both in prayer and the prophetic, and the anointing increased as what we were hearing Him tell us grew in frequency, intensity, and specificity.

Over the years, there were prayers for impartation over me personally and over Dyed4you from many different ministries and people. I firmly believe Papa used each of those divine appointments to increase the work He was doing through me and Dyed4you Ministries. But as with any journey, there are key moments where you know with certainty that something has shifted, and we had one such moment in January of 2017. I was connected with June Reinke of Prophetic Light Ministries, and she prayed impartation via a crazy-wonderful four hour phone call during which we were both experiencing spiritual manifestations.

June flows in a strong prophetic gifting and has been bringing forth daily prophetic words for years. I had no expectation that Papa would have me do anything like that, but 52 days later He downloaded a short word apropos of nothing. I was confused at first, trying to determine if it went with a silk or an art word we were in the process of birthing, but it didn't. Finally, I began to understand He was doing something new. This was both exciting and scary, but I consoled myself that I didn't have to feel pressured to do anything daily. I could just write down whatever He said when He said it, and then share it on the blog for our Dyed4you Ministries site. And that's exactly what I did.

An interesting thing happened. Since I was being mindful to ask Him daily what He had for me, He began to give me something every day. Even though I'd relieved myself of the pressure of doing a daily word, apparently that was what He had in mind. It was a bit like manna. He'd give one nugget a day and two on Saturday because He knew I wasn't a morning person, so getting one before our early church service wasn't going to happen!

As days turned into months, the daily downloads began to take on a format and a flow, and people were being blessed and encouraged (and sometimes challenged) via the words whether they subscribed to them on our website (where we've nicknamed them Prophetic Nuggets), followed us on Facebook, or received a Dyed4you art or silk word that quoted one. Then through a trusted friend and prayer partner, Papa began nudging me toward publishing them in a devotional book. And when I didn't respond to that nudging in a timely enough fashion,

He turned up the volume by having person after person contact me with the suggestion that these downloads should be put into a devotional book and finally connecting me with a publisher. As I like to say, sometimes God is not subtle!

Having given that bit of history, I invite you to let the downloads He's imparted on my journey inspire a journey of your own. Allow the truths contained in these nuggets to challenge and encourage you. I strongly urge you to begin a journal if you don't already have one. Make it something easy to use and accessible. (I can access mine from my phone so it's always with me.) Begin journaling the questions you have for God as well as the thoughts and downloads you get from Him along the way. And you will get downloads because He loves to show Himself to His children.

But we have a key responsibility in this process. Let me explain by giving an example. Assume you have two people who have made a request of you. Both are ones you've granted favors to in the past, but one didn't notice or acknowledge when you fulfilled their request, while the other not only saw and noted it, but thanked you as well. So when they both return with a new request whose are you more likely to grant?

Make no mistake. I'm not implying that you should attempt to manipulate God or that you give thanks just for the purpose of getting more from Him. Rather I'm saying that by behaving in a way that is proper and gracious, you position yourself for blessing. In the same way earthly parents reward the behavior they want to reinforce, so does God.

Being attentive so you can take note when He answers your prayers and questions is wise and loving. And ultimately, that is probably most like the person you are striving to be.

If at this point you aren't sure you hear Him, that's ok! This is a great way to start. By just taking note of questions and what you think you're hearing as answers, you will begin to see patterns as well as His fingerprints. He will find a way to ensure that you're hearing Him and to have you know that you are. For those who feel like they struggle with hearing Him, remember that His ability to speak outweighs your ability to miss Him. It's all about yielding to Him and trusting Him to do the rest.

There are many benefits to journaling, but here are a few good ones to note.

- **It helps you remember**. You will find you remember things better when you take the time to write them out, whether by hand or typing.

- **It increases your ability to see God at work in your life**. As you journal your thoughts, questions, prayers, etc., you will find God responding to them. This allows you to clearly see Him moving in your life.

- **It strengthens your belief.** You become more conscious of His responses when you are taking the time to document them. Through this you will have testimonies, which you can also note. Having all these things written down and dated is a great way to track things so you can clearly see answered prayer, which strengthens your belief in God.

- **It hones your ability to hear**. As you see and document His responses, you will find patterns in how He answers you. This then strengthens your ability to hear Him and your confidence in doing so.

- **It encourages your walk with God and your focus on Him**. Seeing the consistent replies to your questions as well as answers to your prayers encourages you in your walk with God and testifies to His faithfulness. When you journal, you will begin to keep an eye out for His responses in your life. And because you are being mindful to watch, it actually increases your focus on God.

- **It shores up your defenses**. With all the documented evidence of His faithfulness, it becomes easier to stand fast in the face of the enemy's attacks. Each answered question and prayer in your journal is a testimony. And each testimony builds your arsenal and strengthens your defenses, your shield of faith.

I have experienced all these benefits. I use my journal as an arsenal of weapons. That way when the enemy lies to me about God's character or my faith is challenged, I can simply click on my "answered prayer" tag in my journal, which I keep via a private blog, and remind myself of years worth of fulfilled promises. There's a reason I can say with full confidence that He is faithful! And often, when I go back and reread things He's shared, I will get fresh revelation that teaches me even more. These reserves are where much of the inspiration behind the nuggets is flowing from.

So as you begin this journey, get prepared. Be expectant. Set up your method for journaling, and set aside time to do so. I hope you will join me in this journey and encourage yourself in His faithfulness. Bless you as you seek Him and may you hear His voice with increased volume and clarity.

※ ※ ※

Daily Downloads from Heaven

Olam Zeroa (Everlasting Arms)

Beloved, you are precious in My sight. Never forget My love for you or let your circumstances or the world at large cause you to question it. It is firm. Solid. Everlasting. I AM Olam Zeroa, the Everlasting Arms. You are forever wrapped tightly in My embrace. Feel My love, precious one. Pause and feel it.

❊ ❊ ❊

Be with Me

Beloved, step into your closet and shut the door. Take a moment to exhale and pause and just rest in Me. Inhale and receive My love, My rest, My refreshing. Resist the urge to allow yourself to be pulled in so many directions that you have nothing left and are running on empty. Remember I AM your source. I AM always right here with you and waiting – ready to fill you and refresh you. Take that moment to pause and just BE with Me. I will meet you there.

❊ ❊ ❊

Fruit from Adversity

I have loved you with an everlasting love, and My eye is ever upon you, for you are so lovely to My gaze. Nothing about you – no aspect of your life or your past – goes unseen by Me, nor am I unfeeling to anything that has wounded you. Each wound you've received I felt even in greater measure, for I treasure you and hold you dear. I would have you NEVER be hurt. And yet, to those wounds I will bring healing, and through those wounds I will bring testimony that speaks of the power of My love. Nothing will be wasted. So hold fast in adversity, I am with you to bring you through, and My love will cause fruit to burst forth from the land plowed by hardships. I bring life in the desert and joy even in the dark places. So again, hold fast. Mourning may last for the night, but joy comes in the morning!

※ ※ ※

God of Justice (Elohiym Mishpat)

> *Psalm 37:28 (VOICE) "Because the Eternal cherishes justice and will not abandon those loyal to Him…"*

Beloved, I am a God of justice. Even My name is justice. For behold, I will see the good rightly divided from the evil, and the righteous rightly divided from the wicked. I AM righteousness itself! My judgment is righteous. I see things rightly and will not fail to do what is right. Therefore, I can be fully trusted to be loyal to those who love Me, to stay true to those whose hearts are steadfast to Me.

Elohiym Mishpat (God of Justice) Isaiah 30:18

※ ※ ※

Take Action: LOVE

> *1 John 4:20-21 (VOICE) If someone claims, "I love God," but hates his brother or sister, then he is a liar. Anyone who does not love a brother or sister, whom he has seen, cannot possibly love God, whom he has never seen. He gave us a clear command, that all who love God must also love their brothers and sisters.*

Beloved, stay in a place of love. If you love Me, love like Me. I know it will not always be easy. I know it will hurt your pride and chafe your flesh, but it reflects Me and will build a beauty of character in you. Make a point not to respond when your flesh rises up. Pause. Step back and see with My eyes. Love where others may tell you that you need to take action… take action: LOVE.

* * *

Guard the Wellspring of Your Heart

I hold your life dear, beloved, and the enemy longs to snatch it from you. Guard the wellspring of your soul, your heart. Know that the enemy comes to steal, kill, and destroy and his gaze is on you. But do not be afraid, for I AM with you and we walk in victory, in truth, and in righteousness. Stand fast and see the deliverance of the Lord.

I AM faithful. I AM true. I AM steadfast and unchanging. You can rely on Me and trust Me with your heart and with your life. I have given My angels charge over you to guard and protect you, and My heavenly hosts will not fail. Amen.

❃ ❃ ❃

Set Your Face Like Flint

> *Isaiah 50:7 (NLT) Because the Sovereign Lord helps me, I will not be disgraced. Therefore, I have set my face like a stone, determined to do his will. And I know that I will not be put to shame.*

Beloved, do not be caught up in circumstances and the things your natural senses may tell you. What I have said will be. I AM faithful and My word is true. Stay fixed on Me, unmoving, not able to be swayed by the things of this world, hearing My voice clearer than any other. Believe, stand in faith, and watch Me move.

I will allow circumstances to stretch your capacity to believe. I would not allow these things if I didn't know that you could withstand and stay strong. So focus your gaze on Me and your heart on My promises, and wait with joy. In your heart you've desired to be able to testify to My power, so don't be surprised when I give you opportunity to stand in faith, beloved. You asked for this. You will withstand and see My glory unfold.

❃ ❃ ❃

The Joy of My Presence

> *Psalm 16:11 (VOICE) Instead, You direct me on the path that leads to a beautiful life. As I walk with You, the pleasures are never-ending, and I know true joy and contentment.*

In My presence is fullness of joy! Receive My presence. Welcome My presence. Make a place for Me. Prepare for Me. I desire to meet with you, to dwell with you. When you are receiving important guests into your home, you prepare: clean and tidy up your home and your person. In the same way, intentionally carve out time, quiet your internal landscape, still your mind, set aside distractions, and make room for Me. My presence is a gift to you. One that brings peace and joy, refreshing and wholeness. It is not a "quick fix", but a relationship built over time that bears much fruit. Prepare a place for Me, beloved, and I will come.

※ ※ ※

I Desire for You to Flourish

> *1 John 3:4 (AMP) Everyone who practices sin also practices lawlessness; and sin is lawlessness [ignoring God's law by action or neglect or by tolerating wrongdoing—being unrestrained by His commands and His will].*

Beloved, I have shared My will, My instructions, in My word. Do not deceive yourself or allow others to deceive you that I somehow do not mean what I say. I have provided these boundaries for you because I LOVE you. Not to restrain or exert My control over you, but because I KNOW the effect that not following them has, and I desire better for you. I desire for you to flourish and prosper. Align with My will and My instructions, and watch blessing pour forth. For I have promised that if you heed My voice, blessings will come upon you and overtake you.

My will is not a mystery. I have made it clearly known. I invite you and welcome you to know Me more. Read My word and allow My Spirit to guide and teach you. I LONG to be known by you. If you poured out your heart in a love letter, you'd desire that it be read and cherished, for it is your heart on paper. No one who bares their soul in such a way wants to be rejected or ignored. In the same way, I have laid My heart bare before you. Come and know Me more, beloved, for My heart for you is love. I yearn to see you blessed and flourishing! Walk in My ways.

❉ ❉ ❉

Undignified Worship

> *Psalm 45:11 (GW) The king longs for your beauty. He is your Lord. Worship him.*

Beloved, seek My face. Pour your heart out before Me. Your offering will not be wasted for I adore you. You are the apple of My eye. I cannot get enough of you, and just as a parent cherishes every scribbled drawing their beloved child brings them, so I love every offering of praise you bring Me.

So hold nothing back. Worship Me with abandon. Dance, sing, wave your banners, be undignified and unashamed, for the outpouring of your heart ministers to Mine; you undo Me!

❊ ❊ ❊

I Go Before You

> *Exodus 13:21-22 (AMP) The [presence of the] Lord was going before them by day in a pillar (column) of cloud to lead them along the way, and in a pillar of fire by night to give them light, so that they could travel by day and by night. He did not withdraw the pillar of cloud by day, nor the pillar of fire by night, from going before the people.*

I go before you, beloved. I make your way clear. There is no strain on you to lead. Simply follow me as I mark the path. I bring shade to you by day and light to you by night. Stay in step with Me. Do not move without My presence. If the sun burns too brightly or the night looms too dark, you will know you've wandered from Me. I've made it so you can feel the difference; just pause and let yourself feel it.

I want you to follow My lead, beloved, so I've made doing so as easy as possible. Don't overthink it or try to complicate matters by second guessing yourself and wondering whether you're accurately hearing Me or sensing Me; I will let you know if you move off course when your heart is to follow. So rest and trust Me.

❈ ❈ ❈

Testifying Without a Word

> *1 John 2:4 (VOICE) If someone claims, "I am in an intimate relationship with Him," but this big talker doesn't live out His commands, then this individual is a liar and a stranger to the truth.*

A man who is unfaithful to his marriage vows, yet holds himself up as a paragon of a husband is a liar and a hypocrite. Be mindful then, beloved, not to do the same. In humility, read and study My word, walk it out, and let the light of My love reflect from your face just as Moses' did when he spent time with Me. You need not declare your relationship with Me to the world, for My touch on you – the glow of my presence – will be apparent without you saying a word.

The light of your countenance will testify. The strength of your love will testify. The beauty of your compassion will testify. And the depth of your mercy will testify. All of these are a reflection of Me, My touch on your life. No words are needed. The strength of your actions – your very life – testify of Me and Who I AM to you.

❈ ❈ ❈

Your Life is in My Hands

> *Exodus 14:20 (VOICE) The cloud pillar took its position between Egypt's and Israel's camps. The cloud cast darkness by day yet it lit up the sky by night. As a result, the Egyptians never got close to the Israelites the entire night.*

For, behold, My presence protects and guards you. You don't have to worry who has you covered because the answer is Me. It is I who will defend you. Do not step into My path to try to "help," for in doing so you are simply taking matters into your own hands. The things that concern you concern Me. Your life is in My hands. You placed it there when you gave your life to Me. Trust Me to cover you.

Your reputation is Mine, and I have said that every tongue that rises against you will be judged (Isaiah 54:17); beloved, do not defend yourself to others. That is My job and I do it happily. Simply keep your eyes fixed on Me and My call for your life; walk it out and leave the rest to Me.

> *Isaiah 54:17 (VOICE) But no instrument forged against you will be allowed to hurt you, and no voice raised to condemn you will successfully prosecute you. It's that simple; this is how it will be for the servants of the Eternal; I will vindicate them.*

❊ ❊ ❊

Do Not Be Distracted By the "Good"

> *Psalm 127:1 (VOICE) Unless the Eternal builds the house, those who labor to raise it will have worked for nothing. Unless the Eternal stands watch over the city, those who guard it have wasted their time.*

Beloved, don't waste your efforts on things I have not called you to, expending your energy and leaving yourself too worn out to complete the tasks to which you have been assigned. If the enemy cannot stop you from doing good, he will try to deplete your energy and divide your vision by putting "good" things in your path to keep you from the things I have called you to put your efforts and energy to. Stick to your call. Stay aligned with My perfect will. There will always be more "good" things to turn your time and efforts to than you could possibly begin to complete.

Do not be distracted or emotionally manipulated into doing things I have not called you to. In doing these things, not only do you misuse the resources I've given you, but you block the path of the one I HAVE called to do that "good" thing. So step out of the way. Be ok with saying no, trusting that all those involved want you only where I want you. If they don't, THEY are out of alignment, not you, and that isn't for you to fix. You showing by your example that following My will and trusting Me to put everyone in their right place encourages others to do the same.

❈ ❈ ❈

Right Perspective

> *Ephesians 6:10-11 (VOICE) Finally, brothers and sisters, draw your strength and might from God. Put on the full armor of God to protect yourselves from the devil and his evil schemes.*

Draw from Me, beloved. I AM your strength. I AM your might. I AM power and authority. You are not alone out in a storm. I AM with you, beside you. So command the storm to be still, beloved, in My name, and whether the external or internal landscape changes, strength and peace are yours.

Gird up your loins. Without hiding My word in your heart you are defenseless, beloved. So eat it as though it were the choicest of meats bringing you strength and stamina because it does and it will. Know Me. Encourage yourself in the faith by seeing Me more and more for who I AM. Magnify Me in your own eyes and realize that the enemy is no match for Me. As you know Me, you will be able to quiet your soul against the taunts of the enemy because you will know – TRULY know – that I AM greater. I AM.

※ ※ ※

Heart After Me

> *1 Samuel 13:14 (TLV) …Adonai has sought for Himself a man after His own heart…*

I AM searching, beloved, for the ones who will choose Me above all else. The ones whose eyes are fixed on Me and whose hearts are aligned with Mine. Pursue Me, beloved. Lay everything else down and choose Me. Not for what you think I can do for you, but simply because I AM. If you know My heart, you know I AM worth the cost and the effort. And though I love you beyond measure I will not talk you into choosing Me because in the end it must be your choice if it is to mean anything. And so I simply extend My hand to you and ask, "Will you have a heart after Me?"

※ ※ ※

Tune in to My Voice and Hold Fast to My Truth

Ephesians 6:17 (AMP) And take the helmet of salvation...

Beloved, the enemy is a liar and the father of lies. His desire is to debilitate you with fear and doubt and unbelief. Do not listen to him. Remember who you are to Me. Remember what I have called you to. Remind yourself of My promises and My truth. I AM love and I love you with an everlasting love that can never change. Do not let the enemy tell you differently.

Do not concern yourself with the fact that you hear his whispers (of course you do, for he is working at all times towards your demise) but rather focus your efforts and energies on Me and My promises that his whispers will be of no avail. Force them into a position of powerlessness by being so secure in My truth that you are unshakable.

This, beloved, is your helmet of salvation. Your mind protected from his onslaught, his thought-bombs diffused by My truth. Hold fast and do not waver in your trust in Me and in your knowledge of the truth. Close your ears to his lies, and tune in to My voice as you hold My sayings dear in your heart. I AM truth.

> *2 Corinthians 10:5 (VOICE) We are demolishing arguments and ideas, every high-and-mighty philosophy that pits itself against the knowledge of the one true God. We are taking prisoners of every thought, every emotion, and subduing them into obedience to the Anointed One.*

❈ ❈ ❈

Build Your Arsenal

> *Ephesians 6:17 (AMP) And take...the sword of the Spirit, which is the Word of God.*

Beloved, if you would wield the sword of My Spirit, you must know My Word. There are so many things that clamor for your attention as My Word waits – unchanging and available – for you to feast. Choose to make the time. Choose to know Me – My heart, My ways, My instructions for you – for they are to protect you and bring you blessing and goodness in your life. My Word is worth knowing.

The more of My Word that is hidden in your heart, the stronger and more prepared you are to do battle against the enemy of your soul when he brings his onslaught. He comes to steal, to kill, and to destroy. I come to give you strength. The enemy will often twist My Word, and just as when My Son was tempted in the wilderness and He refuted those lies with Truth – with the Word - so you must be equipped to do the same.

For it is not a question of IF the enemy will lie and twist truths; it is a matter of WHEN. Do not be found defenseless and weak, but rather prepare. Just as a lawyer spends time building his knowledge base so he can make the arguments in court to win the day, likewise spend the time each day to build your arsenal and your strength. Again beloved, My Word is worth knowing. I AM worth knowing.

❈ ❈ ❈

Release Your Sound

> *Romans 8:26 (AMPC) So too the [Holy] Spirit comes to our aid and bears us up in our weakness; for we do not know what prayer to offer nor how to offer it worthily as we ought, but the Spirit Himself goes to meet our supplication and pleads in our behalf with unspeakable yearnings and groanings too deep for utterance.*

Make a sound, beloved. Let it come forth from inside you – whether it be a bursting shout, a mighty roar, or a groan too deep for words. Pour it forth – whether an offering of praise or a tool of intercession. Release what is stirring in your belly, for I have placed it there. Let your sound echo through the heavenlies – breaking strongholds, declaring victory, and ascribing praise.

Do not hold back. Do not let the enemy steal your voice. Do not let concerns of what man may think hinder you from doing, being, and birthing that which you are called to. Break forth! Shout in victory! Let your sound declare it to be so! And so the thing shall be established. Release it! Mighty is your sound.

※ ※ ※

Develop a Taste for Me

> *1 John 2:15 (TLB) Stop loving this evil world and all that it offers you, for when you love these things you show that you do not really love God;*

Beloved, don't be taken in by the bright lights and sparkle of this world. It is all flash and glamour – an illusion, a spell intended to deceive you and make you believe there is something of substance there, of value. But there is not. Feasting on the world's glitter is like trying to sustain life eating cotton candy. There is no true value in it, and it loses its appeal quickly in the face of true need.

You can develop a taste for anything. And doing so will mold your preferences. If you develop a taste for the things of this world, it is what you will crave. You may have even been raised to crave this world. But your tastes can change, and you can change them intentionally.

My Word and My Kingdom were meant to sustain. They have true substance. I AM what your soul needs to be satisfied; anything else is just filler and an ineffective substitute. Develop a taste for Me.

❈ ❈ ❈

Seek Peace and Harmony

> *1 Corinthians 1:10 (TLB) But, dear brothers, I beg you in the name of the Lord Jesus Christ to stop arguing among yourselves. Let there be real harmony so that there won't be splits in the church. I plead with you to be of one mind, united in thought and purpose.*

Beloved, seek peace and harmony among the brethren. As you consider others above yourself and extend grace and mercy – seeking to understand, assuming positive intent, and covering in prayer your brothers and sisters in Christ – you will find it easy to operate with My heart and in My love. Pray first, speak second – if at all. Trust My Holy Spirit to do the work in each other's hearts. Each of you is responsible for your own personal growth, and My Holy Spirit will show you what areas to work on next. Just as you trust Me to do that in you, trust that I will do the same in others.

Resist the urge to be prideful if I've already addressed an area with you and you're walking in victory in it, but your brother is not. Extend the grace you wanted to receive, use your strengths to cover one another's weaknesses. Truly function as a body. Walking in love and tenderly caring for each other, compensating when one area is weakened or hurt, allowing time for strength and maturity to be built. Love one another, and bear with one another in love.

Lead by example. Even if others walk in pride and point out your weaknesses – exploiting rather than covering – do not respond in kind. Rather walk in humility as My Son did – simply being Who I created Him to be and acting in a way that was pleasing to Me rather than retaliating or trying to defend Himself. Trust Me to cover you when your brethren let you down, but don't stop walking in the manner I have called you to because even if no one else notices, I do.

❊ ❊ ❊

The Roar and the Whisper

> *1 Kings 19:12 (TLB) And after the earthquake, there was a fire, but the Lord was not in the fire. And after the fire, there was the sound of a gentle whisper.*

Beloved, I AM the Lion AND the Lamb. The roar and the whisper. The thunder and the gentle breeze. Stay fluid and surrendered to My flow. Be mindful not to try to box Me in, or to say, "He speaks only this way" or "He speaks only that way." I will not be contained or controlled. I defy definition simply because I AM beyond comprehension. Allow Me to choose the tone, the volume, the message. Let My spirit govern the flow, for I see things you do not and have reasons for everything I do.

Quiet your spirit and stay open, malleable, in an active form of waiting - a state of readiness awaiting a word or a nudge from Me. Keep your wick trimmed and your oil ready, for the call is coming, and you want to be found ready.

❊ ❊ ❊

I AM Your Source of Strength

> *Psalm 30:7 (AMP) By Your favor and grace, O Lord, you have made my mountain stand strong; You hid Your face, and I was horrified.*

Beloved, I will not turn My face from you while your heart and mind are fixed on Me. When you choose Me, I will never desert you. But I love you enough to let you choose. I love you enough to let you walk away – though I will not make it easy for you to do so, hedging your way with thorns and fiercely pursuing you. Though I AM best for you, I will not force you to choose Me; yet I will hope, and I will contend for your affections because you are worth it.

Even in the darkest hour, My heart remains steadfast to you. So lean on Me. Let Me give you strength, be your strength, be the lifter of your head. For I AM Rum Rosh, the Lifter of Your Head. I AM God.

❊ ❊ ❊

Faithful God (El Aman)

> *1 Thessalonians 5:24 (VOICE) For the God who calls you is faithful, and He can be trusted to make it so.*

Beloved, I AM El Aman, the Faithful God. I AM true to My word. I watch over it to see it fulfilled. My promises are YES and AMEN. They are settled. They are done. You can rely on Me. Others may have let you down, but beloved, I am not them. Trust Me. I will bring it to pass.

Trust requires belief, and I AM a rewarder of those who believe that I AM and who diligently seek Me. So simply keep your eyes fixed on Me. I know I say this again and again, but the world is vying for your attention and the enemy desires to distract you – pulling, pulling from every direction – so quietly, again I say, "Keep your heart and eyes fixed on Me."

Don't be discouraged if your gaze has shifted. Simply move it back. Beloved, I would rather you choose Me over and over a hundred times a day than that you blow it once and never try again. I understand, and I love you. Fix your gaze on me and trust.

> *Hebrews 11:6 (NKJV) But without faith it is impossible to please Him, for he who comes to God must believe that He is, and that He is a rewarder of those who diligently seek Him.*

※ ※ ※

The Lord of Breaking Through (Baal-Perazim)

> *Isaiah 43:19 (VOICE) Watch closely: I am preparing something new; it's happening now, even as I speak, and you're about to see it. I am preparing a way through the desert; Waters will flow where there had been none.*

Watch, beloved. I AM doing something new. I AM bringing forth the supernatural in abundance, doing things you have never seen or imagined. Come along with Me and be part of what I AM doing. No matter the circumstances or situation, I can and will make a way – like water in the desert. I AM Baal-Perazim, Lord of breaking through.

Beloved, the supernatural is about to become natural for you. Expect it. Anticipate it. Welcome it. My ways may cause discomfort, but yield to My flow and you will see it come to pass. Get ready. Get ready. Get ready! Be listening. Stay in that place of active waiting – fully expectant, believing and ready – for I will move suddenly. Though the vision tarries, wait for it. It WILL come to pass. It will not tarry.

> *1 Chronicles 14:11 (AMPC) So [Israel] came up to Baal-Perazim, and David smote the [Philistines] there. Then David said, God has broken my enemies by my hand, like the bursting forth of waters; therefore they called the name of that place Baal-Perazim (Lord of breaking through).*

> *Habakkuk 2:3 (NKJV) For the vision is yet for an appointed time; But at the end it will speak, and it will not lie. Though it tarries, wait for it; Because it will surely come, It will not tarry.*

❊ ❊ ❊

Glimpse of Eternity

> *Genesis 1:2 (NKJV) The earth was without form, and void; and darkness was on the face of the deep. And the Spirit of God was hovering over the face of the waters.*

Beloved, I AM the Creator, and you are made in My image. I have made you to pour forth life, to create. Just as before the creation there was a moment when My Spirit simply hovered, so there will be that moment for you. So wait for it, beloved. I will whisper to your heart. Listen for it. Don't move without Me. I love to create with you.

As you create, beloved, reflect My heart. I will give you ways to express supernatural things in earthly mediums. My heart is for My people to know – truly know and understand – their real home, for you are simply sojourners here. As My people are able to catch the vision, they are better able to stay fixed on my worldview rather than being drawn in by the world's. What a gift that you are able to help others capture that glimpse of eternity!

❊ ❊ ❊

Blessing the Upright

> *Psalm 84:11 (TLB) For Jehovah God is our Light and our Protector. He gives us grace and glory. No good thing will he withhold from those who walk along his paths.*

Beloved, My desire to bless you is far greater than even your desire to be blessed. Walk in My ways. Read My Word. Live it. Know it. Love it, for it is a part of Me. Those who know Truth are far less likely to be deceived. Arm yourself. Know Me, beloved. Position yourself for My blessings, for I stand ready with more than you could possibly contain.

Grace and glory come from Me. All promotion (and even demotion) is from My hand. Trust that I AM moving according to your best interests and that of the kingdom.

> *1 Chronicles 29:11-12 (NLT) Yours, O Lord, is the greatness, the power, the glory, the victory, and the majesty. Everything in the heavens and on earth is yours, O Lord, and this is your kingdom. We adore you as the one who is over all things. Wealth and honor come from you alone, for you rule over everything. Power and might are in your hand, and at your discretion people are made great and given strength.*

※ ※ ※

Unimpeachable Promises

> *2 Peter 3:9 (GW) The Lord isn't slow to do what he promised, as some people think. Rather, he is patient for your sake. He doesn't want to destroy anyone but wants all people to have an opportunity to turn to him and change the way they think and act.*

Beloved, I do not promise lightly, nor do I neglect My word once given. My promises are ALWAYS delivered. My timing of that fulfillment is what man has always struggled with, and yet time and again I have demonstrated My faithfulness - shown that I AM completely trustworthy. Do not be tempted into a place of doubt, for in your heart of hearts you know that I AM true. My word is steadfast and sure. I AM unchanging - the same yesterday, today, and forever. I AM unimpeachable.

So, beloved, wait patiently for all I have promised, knowing it WILL come to pass, knowing My timing is perfect. Know that if I seem to tarry there is a good purpose in doing so. I love My children and am always acting on their (your) behalf as a Father who adores His children and protects them even as He blesses and rewards them. Trust Me.

※ ※ ※

Resist the Temptation to Doubt

> *Genesis 21:1 (VOICE) The Eternal One kept His promise*

Beloved, I AM not a man that I should lie. Nor the son of man that I should repent. I AM infallible. Unchanging. Steadfast. I always keep My promises. I AM faithful from generation to generation. I AM slandered and accused, yet I remain the same: deeply in love with My people.

Resist the temptation to doubt Me when time goes long and the wait becomes agonizing. My plans and timing are for your good. Wait in patience, trusting Me. Do not make an idol of your desire to understand or demand that I explain Myself to you. Am I not God? Would you sit in judgment of My reasoning? Surely not!

You are My child. My beloved one. My heart towards you is good. Trust Me. Believe in My love, kindness, and affection for you, for when you know – truly know – there is no room to doubt My heart for you. My love for you is that great. Overwhelming. Bask in that love as you wait, knowing I AM true to My word.

> *Numbers 23:19 (GW) God is not like people. He tells no lies. He is not like humans. He doesn't change his mind. When he says something, he does it. When he makes a promise, he keeps it.*

✵ ✵ ✵

Secured in Truth

> *Ephesians 6:14 (AMP) So stand firm and hold your ground, having tightened the wide band of truth*

> *(personal integrity, moral courage) around your waist...*

Beloved, My word is truth. Just as you cannot decide to wear "part" of a belt, it is fruitless to choose which parts of My word you will obey while discarding parts you don't like, want, or understand. It leaves you defenseless. Choose ALL of Me. ALL of My word. My Holy Spirit will guide you in walking out that choice, but you must be the one to choose.

Everything hinges on this choice. Just as all other pieces of the armor connect to and rely on the belt, so every part of your life and walk hinges on your choice to secure yourself in truth. It is a central, foundational, core choice. Will you choose Me – My word – without exception or compromise? And if you already have, will you be steadfast in walking that choice out? For this choice takes courage and dauntlessness of heart. Choose wisely, beloved. Arm yourself well.

※ ※ ※

Do Not Lose Heart

> *Psalm 56:8 (VOICE) You have taken note of my journey through life, caught each of my tears in Your bottle...*

Beloved, you are not unseen. I am not heartless to your cries. Every tear you shed is precious to Me. Your heart is precious to Me. I see it all, and am with you through it all. Beloved, do not lose heart. Resist the temptation to throw in the towel. Though you may not have My perspective, know that I am seeing the true impact of your tears, and they are watering your harvest.

Each tear is like a small prayer, a groan of your heart too deep for words. Do not underestimate their power. Just as a tiny seed can grow into a huge tree, so each of your small tears can have weight far beyond what their size might imply. So stay the course, fix your eyes and heart on Me, and trust that all things are working together for good.

❊ ❊ ❊

Kisses of My Mouth

> *Song of Solomon 2:4 (AMP) "He has brought me to his banqueting place, And his banner over me is love [waving overhead to protect and comfort me].*

I cover you with My love, shielding and cocooning you. Protecting, encouraging, nurturing, and restoring you with My presence and the fervency of My devotion. I nourish you with the sweetest of kisses from My mouth. Pause, beloved, and feel My love overtake you. Nothing have I withheld from you. The depths of My heart for you are incalculable, so do not try to measure it, simply receive it as the gift it is. Let it be sustenance to your weary soul.

Watch for My kisses from heaven as I move in your life and the world around you. I AM leaving love notes for you everywhere, simply pay attention and find them. Notice even the most minute details I have aligned to demonstrate My love for you. Whether it be in the rainbows and flowers that bring a smile, or the butterfly in a moment you needed to be reminded of beauty - the rainy nights that sooth your soul, or the vibrant sunshine that warms your heart, I AM here and I AM moving. I AM moving all around you. See Me. My heart is on display.

※ ※ ※

I Will Guide You

> *Isaiah 30:21 (TLB) And if you leave God's paths and go astray, you will hear a voice behind you say, "No, this is the way; walk here."*

Beloved, you will not "accidentally" walk away from Me. I will not force you to stay, but you can't "lose" Me. My desire for you to walk uprightly is even greater than yours, so if your heart is to walk with Me and in My ways, I will help you along that path. I will guide you with My eye, hedge the way you should not go with thorns, and gently direct you along the way. Listen for My voice, beloved, for I AM speaking to you.

So walk with confidence and assurance, knowing the God of all creation is at your side, directing and guiding you. Do not turn to the left or the right or be distracted by the things vying for your attention, stay with Me. Stay righteous. Stay true. Walk in victory.

> *Psalm 32:8 (NKJV) I will instruct you and teach you in the way you should go; I will guide you with My eye.*
>
> *Hosea 2:6 (AMP) "Therefore, behold, I [the Lord God] will hedge up her way with thorns; And I will build a wall against her [shutting off her way] so that she cannot find her paths.*

❈ ❈ ❈

Shine

> *Isaiah 60:1 (ESV) Arise, shine, for your light has come, and the glory of the LORD has risen upon you.*

Beloved, everywhere you look is My glory. The evidence of My touch surrounds you like a hug from heaven, giving witness of My reality so I cannot be denied. And not only does My glory surround you in My creation, but it is IN you – you who were created in My image – and you are the jewel in My crown, bursting forth in glory and beauty as you surrender your life to Me and your will to Mine.

As you yield yourself to Me, My glory shines in and through you in such a way that all can see and are drawn in to its warmth. Do not hide it away or try to dim it because it intimidates others or incites them to jealousy (because they have yet to surrender to Me thus allowing Me to shine through them too). Be all I have made and anointed you to be, and be it unashamedly and unreservedly. Shine, beloved. Shine.

※ ※ ※

Watch and Wait

> *Exodus 14:14 (AMP) The Lord will fight for you while you [only need to] keep silent and remain calm."*

Beloved, there are moments to take up your sword and fight, and moments to rest and watch Me fight for you. This is the moment to keep silent and watch as I move on your behalf. Am I not God? Am I not sovereign? Is My hand too small? The concerns of your heart are moving Me to action, beloved. Watch and wait.

I AM YHVH Sabaoth (the Lord of Hosts) and the heavenly hosts are at My command. The kingdom of darkness will not stand against us. We move in righteousness and light. And darkness cannot overcome the light, but rather light overtakes the darkness. So shall I, the One who created light, overtake the adversary and the kingdom of darkness. Watch and wait.

Quiet your spirit as you wait. Pray. Stand in agreement with Me. Align your heart with Me as you rest and trust. You are in My hand and there is no place safer for you. As an impassioned Father, I AM moving on your behalf. Watch and wait.

※ ※ ※

You are Mine

> *2 Corinthians 6:18 (TPT) I will be a true Father to you, And you will be my beloved sons and daughters," says the Lord Yahweh Almighty.*

Beloved, I have adopted you and claimed you as My own. You are Mine and I am yours. You are accepted and not rejected, loved and not ignored, and treasured not marginalized. You matter to Me on a deep level. I call you My own.

It is My responsibility to protect you and provide for you. Stay under My wing and let Me. Don't struggle against Me or push away simply because others have let you down. I'm not them. And in moments when you feel as if I've let you down, quietly trust that I AM working on your behalf even when you can't see it.

You are Mine, beloved. I do not take that lightly. I cherish you. You are My beloved one. Let Me lavish you with My love.

❈ ❈ ❈

Sweet Nothings

> *Zephaniah 3:17 (AMPC) The Lord your God is in the midst of you, a Mighty One, a Savior [Who saves]! He will rejoice over you with joy; He will rest [in silent satisfaction] and in His love He will be silent and make no mention [of past sins, or even recall them]; He will exult over you with singing.*

Beloved, My love for you knows no bounds. Even as I rejoice over you – exulting, feeling triumphant joy – I also quietly reflect on the miracle that is you, the beauty as you offer your heart to Me. Beloved, My joy cannot be contained. It overflows in songs of love and deliverance. The past is gone, removed as far as the east is from the west, and I simply lean in toward you and whisper sweet nothings, murmurings of love. Will you hear Me? Will you take time to quiet your heart and listen?

A melody of heaven echoes around you, My precious one. Like a sweet, warm breeze on a pleasant summer evening, the sounds surround you and will lull you into that shalom-filled rest if you will let it. Quiet joy, exuberant joy, exceeding peace, and love beyond comprehension. Take My hand, beloved, and hear My whisperings. Know My heart. Feel My love.

❋ ❋ ❋

I AM Your Shelter

> *James 1:2-3 (TLV) Consider it all joy, my brethren, when you encounter various trials, knowing that the testing of your faith produces endurance.*

Beloved, don't shy away from hardships; rather seek Me in the midst of them. I AM the One who calms the storms and brings peace. I AM the One who brings beauty from ashes. Look to Me. I AM your ever-present help in times of trouble and I AM always with you. Quiet your spirit and seek Me. I

AM your shelter in the storm, your cleft in the rock. And I AM working all things for good. I AM.

❊ ❊ ❊

Bear Fruit

> *Galatians 5:22-23 (AMP) But the fruit of the Spirit [the result of His presence within us]...*

Beloved, dwell with Me. Let My Spirit do its work in you. A plant without water will not flourish. It will die. Allow the water of My Spirit to refresh and bring forth life in and through you. If you abide with Me, you cannot help but bear fruit. And that fruit will be abundant and visible to all. It will be sweet, and it will teach others of Me without you saying a word. You will simply reflect Me and My character.

Stay in My presence. Choose to hover there. In these periods of gestation, I AM growing beautiful things in you. Let them come to full term. Let them mature. Take your time with Me. There are blessings that only come in My presence and I desire those for you greatly. Come be with Me and see what comes forth as a result.

> *John 15:4 (AMP) Remain in Me, and I [will remain] in you. Just as no branch can bear fruit by itself without remaining in the vine, neither can you [bear fruit, producing evidence of your faith] unless you remain in Me.*

❊ ❊ ❊

Alive in His Love {Moments with God}

{my heart cries} You died for us. It's not a myth. It's not a fable. You are alive. You are ALIVE! You rose from the grave after my sins You paid. Hallelujah.

{He responds} I love you, beloved, and you were well worth the cost. I see your sins no more. They are removed as far as the east is from the west. Behold, you are beautiful, My love. Your eyes are like dove's eyes. Made pure – washed clean – in the Blood. Beautiful, My love. Your eyes, they overwhelm Me. You think I overwhelm you, but you overwhelm Me! My love for you defies description. My heart is for you. I AM steadfast and true. My love for you unchanging. Respond to Me. Melt into Me. Yield. I AM safe and My love shelters, protects, and restores. You are Mine.

{my heart responds} I'm not worthy! How could you love me like that? How can I rest in Your love knowing I'm unworthy?

{with love in His eyes He says} Beloved, it's not about worth or being worthy. This is My choice. It's a gift. Stop trying to earn what has already been given to you! It is yours. Freely and unconditionally. Forever. Unchanging. Open your hand – open your heart – and understand it isn't about being good enough. It's simply about receiving what I'm giving you. I love you, My precious, and that will NEVER change. Receive it and flourish!

{weeping my heart replies} I believe – help me in my unbelief!

{Selah} (Pause and reflect on all that. Let it sink in. Breathe it in.)

{His love pours over me as I wait, hovering in His presence. Washing over me. Flooding my soul. Thick like oil. Deep and rich. Covering me. Saturating me. Healing me. Received.}

❊ ❊ ❊

Do What is Good

> *1 Corinthians 10:23 (NIV) "I have the right to do anything," you say—but not everything is beneficial. "I have the right to do anything"—but not everything is constructive.*

Beloved, I have given you the ability to choose that you might choose well. Choose things that bring life. Choose things that build up. Choose things that foster relationship with Me. Will I force you to make certain choices? No. But don't think for a moment that I don't have a strong opinion on what you should pick or that I am not eagerly waiting to see what decisions you make.

I AM highly vested in you. In the outcome of your life and walk! I love you and desire blessing for you. It's why so much of My word is dedicated to instructing you in right and wrong that you might make informed decisions - choosing that which is good, perfect, and true. Choose Me and the things of Me.

> *Philippians 4:8 (NIV) Finally, brothers and sisters, whatever is true, whatever is noble, whatever is right, whatever is pure, whatever is lovely, whatever is admirable—if anything is excellent or praiseworthy—think about such things.*

❊ ❊ ❊

Love Like Me

> *Galatians 5:22-23 (AMP) But the fruit of the Spirit [the result of His presence within us] is love [unselfish concern for others]…*

Beloved, to be like Me you must walk in love, thinking of others' needs above your own and considering their interests and feelings. Bear with them in love. Take the high road, walking in humility even in moments when your flesh is screaming. Love.

I'm not asking you to let others use or abuse you. There are moments to stand fast, but there are also moments to yield. When your flesh cries to be defensive or offended, instead walk like Me: in love. In understanding. In humility. I AM with you. I will strengthen you. Be known for your love.

> *Ephesians 4:2 (VOICE) Be humble. Be gentle. Be patient. Tolerate one another in an atmosphere thick with love.*

❊ ❊ ❊

Walk Uprightly

> *Ephesians 6:14 (AMP) So stand firm and hold your ground...having put on the breastplate of righteousness (an upright heart),*

Beloved, it matters not if everyone around you compromises their integrity; you know the level to which you are called. Walk in it. Without apology or hesitation. Not because you know I AM with you and see your actions, but because you refuse to lower yourself or compromise your integrity.

Walk in uprightness, setting the example for those around you. You won't need to say a word, rather lead by example. Show them that walking with Me makes you different, not in a self-righteous way, but rather one of quiet humility, compassion, and righteousness.

For I AM strengthening you. What you're called to is not impossible. And in the moments it is difficult, know that it is growing the fruit of the Spirit within you. You can do it. I AM with you and I strengthen you. Do not give the enemy a toehold. But in the moments you fall short, quickly repent and right yourself. Uprightness protects your heart, beloved, and your heart is most precious to Me. Guard it well.

❊ ❊ ❊

Eyes on the Throne

> *Isaiah 6:1 (TLB) ...I saw the Lord! He was sitting on a lofty throne, and the Temple was filled with his glory.*

Beloved, do not lose sight of Who I AM - the brilliance of My majesty, the grandeur of My glory. It is not in pride or arrogance that I tell you to keep your thoughts fixed on this, but rather so your vision will be rightly aligned. My hand is not too small nor My arm too short to address any issue that comes your way. The heavens and earth are My creation, and I AM sovereign. I AM bigger than you know. No problem can look large in comparison to Me.

So let My glory overwhelm you and fill your eyes with My splendor. Know Who it is that is on your side, for I AM for you and not against you. I AM the Lord of Hosts – YHVH Sabaoth – and there are far more for you than there are against you. Do not let the enemy tempt you to discouragement and defeat simply by his taunts. He is a liar and the father of lies. I AM truth and I rule in righteousness. As when a child tries to fight a grown man, there may appear to be a struggle, but in the end there is no question of who will win.

❊ ❊ ❊

Hear Me Roar

> *Proverbs 19:12 (VOICE) A king's rage is like the thunderous roar of a lion, but his favor is like a cooling mist upon the grass.*

Beloved, I fiercely love My children. I jealously guard them and have set My hosts around them to protect and battle on their behalf. You are Mine – My anointed people – and I roar over you. Do you not hear the sound? It reverberates through the heavens; and for everyone in that realm, there is no doubt you are under My protection.

Trust that I AM covering you. Even when you don't see it, I AM thwarting the enemy's plans left and right, protecting you from unseen dangers and traps. I AM covering you. I AM your rear guard and I go before you. I conquer the enemy and his attacks by day, and rebuke the enemy and his terrors by night. I AM with you and you are Mine.

> *Psalm 105:15 (VOICE) "Do not lay a hand on My anointed people; do not do any harm to My prophets."*

> *Psalm 91:11 (AMPC) For He will give His angels [especial] charge over you to accompany and defend and preserve you in all your ways [of obedience and service].*

※ ※ ※

See Me

> *Romans 1:20 (AMPC) For ever since the creation of the world His invisible nature and attributes, that is, His eternal power and divinity, have been made intelligible and clearly discernible in and through the things that have been made (His handiworks). So [men] are without excuse [altogether without any defense or justification],*

Beloved, stop to look around you. See Me in My creation. I AM everywhere. My fingerprints surround you. Evidence of My existence. Evidence of My wisdom. Evidence of My creativity. Evidence of My design. Evidence of Me. See Me.

See Me and see My character. See how I have provided for the smallest of creatures and seen to even the tiniest details. And My creation isn't just functional, it is beautiful too. It is there to be appreciated and enjoyed – a feast for the senses, sumptuous, glorious, and breathtaking. It is all an extension of Me. My creation points to Me. See Me in it and know Me more.

❊ ❊ ❊

What's Mine is Yours

> *Luke 15:31 (ESV) And he said to him, 'Son, you are always with me, and all that is mine is yours.*

All that's Mine is yours, and all that's yours is Mine. Just as you surrendered all to Me when you gave

Me your heart, beloved, so all I have is yours. As you align with Me and we walk in unity, there is no lack. For I AM with you. Rest in Me. Let Me lead you, guide you, and direct you. Let Me position you for blessing. Stay yielded to Me.

Move with My Spirit as we walk together, trusting Me to steer you rightly. If your heart is to hear Me and do My will, I will make sure you're accurately understanding My instructions. Trust Me. Trust Me and obey. Position yourself for blessing. Stay in step with Me and pliable to My Spirit's leading. Be expectant, knowing I AM a good Father who loves His children. I AM faithful.

> *Psalm 37:25-26 (VOICE) Through my whole life (young and old), I have never witnessed God forsaking those who do right, nor have I seen their children begging for crumbs, Because they are always giving and sharing; truly, their children are a joyful blessing.*

✻ ✻ ✻

Worth the Price

> *1 Peter 1:18-19 (VOICE) You know that a price was paid to redeem you from following the empty ways handed on to you by your ancestors; it was not paid with things that perish (like silver and gold), but with the precious blood of the Anointed, who was like a perfect and unblemished sacrificial lamb.*

Beloved, you were worth the price though it was steep. You are that precious to Me. I want you to understand the depths of My love for you. I want you to understand your value. At the same time, I want you to understand what your sin cost because I want to see you choose wisely going forward. Though My grace is freely given, it isn't free. It has a cost, a great one. You are simply worth it.

But do not fall prey to the enemy's lies that a "small sin" here or a "little lie" there makes no difference. Beloved, you have been washed clean. Don't be coerced back into the muck and the mire. Walk in integrity and righteousness. Choose wisely and exercise discernment. Do not trample the gift you've been given by treating it as though it has no value. Walk rightly and let your walk challenge others to do the same. Encourage one another in uprightness and love. Boldly be different from the world and do so unapologetically, for this is not your home. Don't try to fit in. You belong with Me and you are Mine.

> *Isaiah 53:10 (KJV) Yet it pleased the Lord to bruise him; he hath put him to grief: when thou shalt make his soul an offering for sin, he shall see his seed, he shall prolong his days, and the pleasure of the Lord shall prosper in his hand.*
>
> *John 15:19 (NLT) The world would love you as one of its own if you belonged to it, but you are no longer part of the world. I chose you to come out of the world, so it hates you.*

✽ ✽ ✽

Do Not Hesitate

> *Ephesians 3:12 (AMPC) In Whom, because of our faith in Him, we dare to have the boldness (courage and confidence) of free access (an unreserved approach to God with freedom and without fear).*

Beloved, do not hesitate. Approach Me with confidence knowing My desire is for you and My heart longs to know your heart more. Share your secrets with Me and your hopes and dreams. They are safe here. YOU are safe here. Loved unconditionally. What matters to you matters to Me.

So bring your requests and supplications. I will hear and respond. Trust Me to know what is best to do, but trust Me with your desires regardless of whether you think I'll fulfill them or not. I cherish your thoughts. I happily carry your burdens (Cast all your cares on Me!). I AM with you, beside you, always.

> *Psalm 37:4 (ESV) Delight yourself in the Lord, and he will give you the desires of your heart.*

❉ ❉ ❉

Shift Your Understanding of Who You Are

> *Ephesians 1:6 (KJV) To the praise of the glory of his grace, wherein he hath made us accepted in the beloved.*

Beloved, you are no longer alone. You are grafted in, a part of My family – a part of Me. Adopted. Accepted. Beloved. Your DNA has changed – your fundamental makeup. See what I see. See rightly. Align your sense of self with how I see you. My Spirit dwells in you, and as you abide in My presence My glory reflects in your countenance.

Do not grow weary of My presence or allow it to become commonplace or valueless. My presence is a gift, a blessing, a resting place for your heart. In My presence you are healed, refreshed, restored, made whole. As you dwell with Me a deep sense of belonging takes root in your heart as My thoughts and actions repeatedly demonstrate who you are – that you are precious and prized. Allow My heart towards you to shift your own understanding of who you are. Align your view with Mine. You are safe with Me.

※ ※ ※

Higher Than Any Created Thing

> *Jeremiah 29:13 (NLT) If you look for me wholeheartedly, you will find me.*

Love Me, beloved. Choose Me. Desire the Creator above the creation or created things. See Me. Know Me. Recognize My fingerprints. Creation points to Me. The purpose of its glory and grandeur and even its intricate design is to help you know Me. I AM higher than any created thing. It all points to Me.

I AM engaging you. I AM drawing you in. Come to Me and choose Me. Don't be distracted by the things around you. Let the world fall away. Stay in a place of shalom – the peace that wars against chaos. Let it quiet the storms. Find Me there in that place of peace. Seek Me. When you seek Me with all your heart you will find Me. I want to be found by you. I AM drawing you in and drawing you closer. Run to Me, beloved. Enjoy Me and let us enjoy life together.

※ ※ ※

I AM Trustworthy

> *Psalm 100:5 (TPT) For the Lord is always good And ready to receive you. He's so loving that it will amaze you, So kind that it will astound you! And He is so famous for His faithfulness toward all. Everyone knows our God can be trusted, For He keeps His promises to every generation!*

Beloved, I AM faithful. From generation to generation I AM the same – steadfast and trustworthy. I keep My promises. My word does not return void. It accomplishes its purpose. For I watch over it to make certain it does, so important is My integrity to Me. I can be trusted. I AM trustworthy. I AM worthy of your confidence. I AM safe. I will always receive you. I will not turn My face from you. Take My hand and rest in My word and the truth of it.

Be like Me. Let your word be your bond. Do not give it lightly, and honor that which you've said.

Reflect Me. Reflect My character. Help the world know Me by seeing you. You are made in My image and likeness, and My Spirit resides within you. This is not too hard for you. Even the little things matter. Your integrity is exemplified by choices made when no one is looking. Walk in righteousness, beloved. Let your actions glorify Me.

※ ※ ※

Equip Yourself

> *Ephesians 6:13 (AMP) Therefore, put on the complete armor of God, so that you will be able to [successfully] resist and stand your ground in the evil day [of danger]...*

Beloved, being dressed for battle does not ensure it will come; it simply ensures you're ready and equipped if and when it does. Yes, I protect you, cover you, and fight for you, but you must also be prepared to fight for yourself. Beloved, you still choose what thoughts you entertain and what things you welcome into your space, so you must choose wisely. And when the enemy comes, stand and resist. Then we can stand together – united – working toward a common cause.

When the enemy lies, recognize it for what it is and reject that lie. When he tempts you to compromise, see the slippery slope for what it is and stand fast. Be alert for his ploys and thwart them at every turn. The more you know the truth – My word – the easier it is to see his evil manipulations. Equip yourself, beloved, and be prepared, but know I AM with you always.

❊ ❊ ❊

I AM the Way Maker

> *Ephesians 6:13 (AMP) ...and having done everything [that the crisis demands], to stand firm [in your place, fully prepared, immovable, victorious].*

Beloved, there are moments to fight, but there are moments where all that is left to do is stand fast. You've prepared, you're equipped, you're positioned. It's time to simply be immovable and leave the rest to Me. Knowing you have all of heaven behind you – the hosts ready and willing to fight on your behalf – be steadfast.

This is the test of faith. To stand at the Red Sea with an enemy bearing down on you, and to trust the One who is trustworthy to make a way where there seems to be no way. I AM the way maker. I part the seas. Stand in faith allowing your stance to declare your confidence in your God – in Me. I will not let you down. I will meet you in that place for I AM faithful and I bring victory in My mighty hand.

❊ ❊ ❊

Blaze Forth

> *Matthew 5:14-15 (VOICE) And you, beloved, are the light of the world. A city built on a hilltop cannot be hidden. Similarly it would be silly to light a lamp and then hide it under a bowl. When someone lights a lamp, she puts it on a table or a desk or a chair, and the light illumines the entire house.*

Beloved, let your fervor and your zeal pour forth like a rising flood, refining, bringing life, bringing refreshing, bringing healing. Resist the temptation to diminish who you are to make others more comfortable. For I have created you perfectly, exactly how I have intended you to be, and it is good. Blaze forth! Shining in all your glory. Reflecting Me. Let your passion fire ignite those around you. Spark them into roaring flames.

Your light overtakes the darkness, not the reverse. The darkness cannot overtake you for the radiance of My glory shines forth and nothing can make it dim. So burn brightly and in doing so give others permission to do the same.

❋ ❋ ❋

Sober Responsibility

> *Romans 8:5-8 (The Message) Those who think they can do it on their own end up obsessed with measuring their own moral muscle but never get around to exercising it in real life. Those who trust*

> *God's action in them find that God's Spirit is in them—living and breathing God!...*

Beloved, I have placed a power in you – My Spirit – that cannot be contained or controlled. And you are a vessel that I AM moving through mightily. My authority rests upon you. Move in it unapologetically. I have called you to touch My people and to bring My healing and restoration. You are My hands and feet, reflecting My heart, so that others may know Me and know Me more deeply. This is a weighty responsibility to demonstrate My heart to those who need Me so desperately but it is not a burden for you. It is simply a sober responsibility. But beloved, you wear it lightly, allowing Me to share that weight and simply flowing in My spirit, and it is beautiful. Thank you for allowing Me to move through you in such mighty and powerful ways.

I love you so deeply. But My love for you is not because of your yieldedness and willingness to move on My behalf, but rather simply because you are My precious child. And yet I love partnering with you to change lives. Thank you for being willing to lay yourself bare for the good of others. Walk in the fullness of all I have called you to. My blessing and My hand rest upon you.

✵ ✵ ✵

Align with My Cadence

> *2 Samuel 5:24 (VOICE) When you hear the sound of a mighty army marching, reverberating in the*

tops of the balsam trees, come quickly and fight, for the Eternal has gone ahead of you into battle to destroy the army of the Philistines.

Beloved, listen for My sound. Listen for My heartbeat. Listen for the sound of Me moving – taking action. Tune in your spiritual senses to My frequency so you may be alert to how I AM moving. I want you to know. I do not want you to be surprised. I want you aligned with Me – in step with My cadence – so catch My rhythm and move with Me.

When we align, the results that come forth have supernatural impact. Like when the walls of Jericho fell at the sound of the blasts and the shouts of Israel, when My people align with Me – My heartbeat, My rhythm, My sound – and move with Me, I move in power and darkness trembles. Hear Me, beloved, and move with My sound!

> *Amos 3:7 (TLV) For the Lord Adonai, will do nothing, unless He has revealed His counsel to His servants the prophets.*

> *Joshua 6:20 (ESV) ...As soon as the people heard the sound of the trumpet, the people shouted a great shout, and the wall fell down flat...*

※ ※ ※

I Surround You With My Favor

> *Psalm 5:12 (AMP) For You, O Lord, bless the righteous man [the one who is in right standing with You]; You surround him with favor as with a shield.*

Beloved, you never need to work to earn My favor. You already have it. You are clothed in it. You can focus on walking uprightly and cultivating relationship with Me because My favor isn't anything you need to work for. It is given freely and surrounds you like a shield. I insulate and protect you because you are My beloved one in whom I AM well pleased.

Rest in that favor, knowing it is there for you – covering you – simply because you are Mine. Walk in the confidence that comes from knowing you are loved, cherished, and appreciated, for you are! I delight in you. You are the apple of My eye, My heart's desire – the center of My world. Hear the love songs I sing over you and the sweet words of life and affection that I whisper in your ear. I AM with you always. I will never leave your side. You are priceless to Me. Rest in the safety of that understanding.

※ ※ ※

I AM the Eternal One

> *Revelation 22:13 (AMP) I am the Alpha and the Omega, the First and the Last, the Beginning and the End [the Eternal One]."*

Beloved, I AM omnipresent. I AM everywhere at all times. I AM the first and the last, the beginning and the end – I AM. Never forget Who it is that is for you. Don't let the lies of the enemy of your soul convince you I AM less than… I AM the Eternal One – bigger than you can begin to imagine – and I AM on your side.

May My majesty leave you breathless and My splendor make you stand in awe. Is anything too great for Me? Is anything beyond My reach? Remember My greatness. May I be magnified in your eyes. May you glimpse My glory and begin to have whispers of understanding of how magnificent I AM. If you see Me rightly, the scale of everything and everyone else becomes rightly aligned. Truly greater is He that is for you than he who is against you. I AM God.

> *1 John 4:4 (TLB) Dear young friends, you belong to God and have already won your fight with those who are against Christ because there is someone in your hearts who is stronger than any evil teacher in this wicked world.*

❊ ❊ ❊

Set Apart

> *1 Peter 2:9 (VOICE) But you are a chosen people, set aside to be a royal order of priests, a holy nation, God's own; so that you may proclaim the wondrous acts of the One who called you out of inky darkness into shimmering light.*

Beloved, you are set apart. Chosen. If you feel like you're different and you don't fit in, that's a good thing because I've called you out and made you holy. You are sanctified and whole. A new creation for My pleasure and My glory. Shine brightly, beloved. Make My glory known.

You've been set apart to be with Me and to minister to Me. Sit at My feet as Mary did. Lie against My chest as John did. Hover close, beloved, that we might whisper and dream together. You are My own – My child, My precious one. Resist the temptation to sully yourself or get sucked into habitual sin. Be holy, beloved. Walk differently. You've been washed clean. Sparkle and shine for all to see.

※ ※ ※

Pray for My Kingdom to Come

> *Matthew 6:10 (VOICE) Bring about Your kingdom. Manifest Your will here on earth, as it is manifest in heaven.*

Beloved, remember to pray for My kingdom to come – that My will might be established in the earth. Align with My heart and My plans. Darkness trembles when your prayers align with My will. The prayers of the righteous bring forth tremendous results. I hear your prayers – each and every one. Never hesitate to share your heart with Me for your thoughts are precious to Me.

And, beloved, persist in prayer. Do not grow weary. Let your heart be moved and let My Spirit lead as you pour out your petitions before My throne. I do not take them lightly. When we partner together, the enemy doesn't stand a chance. Let My Spirit move you with compassion. Take the time to bless and pray for those around you. No prayer goes unheard. Even the smallest petition can move My heart. Have eyes to see and ears to hear and join with Me as you pray for heaven to come.

> *James 5:16 (AMP) …The heartfelt and persistent prayer of a righteous man (believer) can accomplish much [when put into action and made effective by God—it is dynamic and can have tremendous power].*

❈ ❈ ❈

Be Free

> *John 10:10 (VOICE) The thief approaches with malicious intent, looking to steal, slaughter, and destroy; I came to give life with joy and abundance.*

Beloved, I AM Palet – your deliverer, your stronghold and safe place. In Me and through Me you are free. Though the enemy seeks to entrap you, deceive you, and weigh you down, you can choose to be free, for you have Me on your side. Though he would drain the life from you and cover your joy with shrouds of depression, I AM with you to save you and deliver you.

Look to Me. Focus on Me. You can be mindful of his ploys enough to thwart them without giving him your focus. Be free! Stay close to Me. I AM your freedom. I AM your joy. I AM your strong tower. I AM the lover of your soul! Cling to Me and rejoice in your freedom, for it is already done. Don't settle for mediocre. I came that you might have abundance! Walk in the fullness of your freedom.

> *Psalm 18:2 (NIV) The Lord is my rock, my fortress and my deliverer; my God is my rock, in whom I take refuge, my shield and the horn of my salvation, my stronghold.*

❊ ❊ ❊

Trust in Me and Soar

> *Isaiah 40:31 (VOICE) But those who trust in the Eternal One will regain their strength. They will soar on wings as eagles. They will run—never winded, never weary. They will walk—never tired, never faint.*

Beloved, soar with Me. If you are feeling weary or faint, lean more on Me. I can take it and I want to take it. I AM your stronghold, your strong tower, your place of safety and rest. Lean on Me and trust in Me. As you press in and trust Me more and more, you are strengthened because I AM your strength.

Yield to My flow and soar with Me. As you trust Me and trust My direction, I will lead you how and where you need. The enemy wants you wasting time on things I have not called you to, allowing the "good" to steal your time and energy so the "best" never has its moment to come. He always tries to wear you out, but that is not of Me. Even I chose rest on the sabbath. Everything has its time and season. Trust Me to know the flow.

❊ ❊ ❊

Tune in to My Frequency

> *Psalm 40:1 (AMP) I waited patiently and expectantly for the Lord; And He inclined to me and heard my cry.*

Beloved, I AM always speaking. Settle your spirit, quiet your soul, and listen. I AM right there, whispering to My beloved one, My precious child, the apple of My eye – you. Be patient. If you had something to share and the person you were speaking to was rushing you, would you feel heard? Important? Respected? You'd want time and an unhurried pace. Leave that same space for Me to speak. If you create the space, I will meet you there.

Be expectant. Trust that I AM speaking to you. Refuse the doubt and unbelief that come to plague you. You know where those lies come from, and it isn't Me. More than you want to hear Me, I desire to be heard. Sit at My feet and wait on Me. Take a deep breath in, and quiet the internal noise. Tune in to My frequency. I AM here. I AM ready. I AM speaking.

※ ※ ※

I AM Limitless

> *Revelation 4:3 (VOICE) The One enthroned gleamed like jasper and carnelian, and a rainbow encircled the throne with an emerald glow.*

Beloved, I AM radiant. Shining in splendor. Enthroned above all. Swirls of color surround me. Light emanates from Me. I AM glorious. See Me and be moved in holy awe. Rightly see Me. Allow your spirit to discern and embrace My throne room. With your spiritual eyes see the glory of this place. Hear the voices crying, "Holy! Holy! Holy!" Understand My grandeur and majesty. Know Me as I AM.

Having seen Me as I truly am, would you try to put Me in a box? Would you try to contain or control Me? Beloved, I cannot be manipulated or controlled. Reject the temptation to make Me smaller so you can fully comprehend Me. I AM beyond comprehension, and that is good. I AM moving in ways you can't see or imagine, and that is good. I AM bigger than you know, and that is good.

I AM limitless! I know no bounds. Nothing is too great for Me, for I AM greater than all. I AM.

❈ ❈ ❈

Carry an Atmosphere of Peace

> *Psalm 5:3 (AMP) In the morning, O Lord, You will hear my voice; In the morning I will prepare [a prayer and a sacrifice] for You and watch and wait [for You to speak to my heart].*

Make time to meet with Me, beloved. Come sit with Me. Wait on Me. Listen for My voice. Start your day with a pause. Allow My shalom – the peace that wars against chaos – to settle in your heart and mind. Start your day in that place of quiet, tuned into My frequency. Learn to find that place quickly and stay there.

Carry that quiet with you throughout your day. The enemy will seek to shatter it, but hold fast to it and to Me. It is your Inheritance, it belongs to you and is your right. He cannot take it away. Only you can release it. So don't let go. Hold fast and walk in peace, shifting the atmosphere around you to align with that peace rather than aligning to its chaos. Find Me in that place and hold on tight, I AM with you always.

❈ ❈ ❈

Be Naked and Unashamed

> *James 5:16 (AMP) Therefore, confess your sins to one another [your false steps, your offenses], and pray for one another, that you may be healed and restored...*

Beloved, do not let pride or shame or fear of judgement keep you from confessing your sins. The enemy desires to keep you in bondage to them, wrapping you tightly in feelings of guilt and shame because he knows your confession will usher in freedom for you and he wants to keep you from it. Don't let him.

Be naked and unashamed, willing to be transparent and vulnerable with your siblings in Christ. Trust that I will protect your heart, and trust that I will move in theirs as they respond to you and pray for you. Allow the fullness of your healing to come. Be restored and fully transformed. Be free.

❊ ❊ ❊

Cultivate Relationship with Me

> *Luke 10:41-42 (GW) The Lord answered her, "Martha, Martha! You worry and fuss about a lot of things. There's only one thing you need. Mary has made the right choice, and that one thing will not be taken away from her."*

Beloved, don't allow yourself to get distracted by busyness. There will always be many good, worthwhile activities, but I have not called you to them all. Relationship with Me is more important than anything you could be doing, so make the time to cultivate it. Choose the better part – time with Me – and it will not be taken from you.

Remember that I AM the vine and you are a branch. I AM your source of life. Draw from Me that you might bear fruit and bear it abundantly. Abide in Me. Dwell and rest in My presence that you might know Me and hear My voice clearly. Then you will know that you know your time is not wasted on fruitless activities because I will direct you. Rest in Me and bear fruit.

> *John 15:5 (AMP) I am the Vine; you are the branches. The one who remains in Me and I in him bears much fruit, for [otherwise] apart from Me [that is, cut off from vital union with Me] you can do nothing.*

※ ※ ※

Create with Me

> *Isaiah 40:28 (TLB) Don't you yet understand? Don't you know by now that the everlasting God, the Creator of the farthest parts of the earth, never grows faint or weary? No one can fathom the depths of his understanding.*

Beloved, I AM the idea maker. I never run out of ideas. My creativity knows no bounds. Take My hand and create with Me. I love to share in the joy of bringing forth new life and ideas into being. I AM the Creator. Listen for My whisper and be moved by the touch of My hand. I declared light into being, and it came forth. Behold the smallest detail on the daintiest flower is My design. I AM beautiful and I bring forth beauty.

I will paint the sky as you paint with words. I will create new colors as you blend your palette. I will bring forth music as you sing a new song. Don't hold back. Don't censor yourself, or restrain or limit your creativity. Allow it to flow and My Spirit to flow through you. Let your work reflect My heart and My kingdom. Bring forth aspects of My glory and My grandeur. Make Me known in the earth.

❊ ❊ ❊

I AM Mighty to Save

> *Zephaniah 3:17 (VOICE) The Eternal your God is standing right here among you, and He is the champion who will rescue you. He will joyfully celebrate over you; He will rest in His love for you; He will joyfully sing because of you like a new husband.*

Beloved, I AM your champion. I fight for your cause. I AM on your side and I AM mighty to save. I snatch your feet from the net, pulling you from the snares of the enemy, saving you because I love you.

Rejoice with Me in your freedom. Hear Me sing over you in love. I AM here. I AM with you, ever by your side. Rest in Me. Lean into Me. Know I

AM here. Look to Me and don't be overwhelmed. I AM where your help comes from. Always remember that. Always remember to look to Me and call out to Me. I AM ever present and ready to fight on your side.

❊ ❊ ❊

A Slave to Bondage No More

> *2 Corinthians 3:17 (AMPC) Now the Lord is the Spirit, and where the Spirit of the Lord is, there is liberty (emancipation from bondage, freedom).*

Beloved, My Spirit brings freedom. Receiving Me is receiving My Spirit. You are a slave to bondage no more. My Spirit lives within you. The traps of the enemy cannot hold you as you surrender yourself to Me. Let My Spirit lead and guide you. Be sensitive to My flow. I will direct you, I will teach you, and I will convict you. Trust Me to lead you rightly, and trust Me to lead others rightly as they surrender to Me too.

I can open the door to your cage, but I cannot force you to fly. You must choose to fly free. I have made a way, but you must walk it out. Beloved, soar with Me. You've been released – the chains broken. Don't believe the enemy's lies that you are still his hostage. The blood has paid the price. You need not try to pay it again, it is already covered. Simply move in the freedom that came at so high a cost.

❊ ❊ ❊

Nurture Your Inner Man

> *Proverbs 31:30 (AMPC) Charm and grace are deceptive, and beauty is vain [because it is not lasting], but a woman who reverently and worshipfully fears the Lord, she shall be praised!*

Beloved, do not be sucked in by vanity, ever chasing fickle trends and the approval of man. Allow the radiance of your countenance to shine, and the soft glow of My presence resting on you to bring forth beauty.

May your heart's focus be on Me, not on the cares of this world. Though, yes, it is right to take care of your outer body and belongings, that should not take precedence over nurturing your inner man in relationship with Me.

So worship Me without reserve. Gaze on My face with reverential awe. Listen keenly for My voice. Rejoice in the wonder of My presence. Be made whole. Be made beautiful.

✣ ✣ ✣

Recharge in My Presence

> *Acts 3:19 (VOICE) So now you need to rethink everything and turn to God so your sins will be forgiven and a new day can dawn, days of refreshing times flowing from the Lord.*

Beloved, take the time to recharge in My presence. You are called to usher in My presence wherever you go, changing the atmosphere around you and reflecting the glory that is Me. You cannot do that effectively if you are wiped out, exhausted, and spiritually dry. Do not run out of oil, beloved, for the oil of My Spirit brings healing and restoration. It is vital to bring life. Keep your oil full, your lamp prepared, and your light shining brightly.

Refresh with Me. Recharge with Me. Let Me refill you, restore and renew you. Rest in Me and let Me have My way in your heart, beloved, for My touch is gentle and My love for you knows no bounds.

> *Matthew 25:4 (GW) The wise bridesmaids, however, took along extra oil for their lamps.*

❊ ❊ ❊

Trust Me to Guide and Provide

> *Haggai 2:8 (NIV) 'The silver is mine and the gold is mine,' declares the Lord Almighty.*

Beloved, the silver and gold are Mine. Wealth and honor come from Me alone. Cease striving in your flesh and look to Me – the Author and Finisher of your faith – to meet your needs. Don't seek man's favor or approval. Seek relationship with Me, and I will give you favor where I would have you have it. I will open doors that cannot be shut for you to walk through, and close the ones where you should not go so that none can open them.

Trust Me to guide and provide. With joy give, and gratitude receive. Follow My lead. Nothing is to hard for Me. Quiet yourself and listen for My voice to instruct you, "this is the way, walk ye in it." I will not lead you astray. Trust My plans and My purpose. Trust Me. I AM mindful of your needs without you saying a word. I AM a good Father.

> *1 Chronicles 29:11-12 (TLB) Yours is the mighty power and glory and victory and majesty. Everything in the heavens and earth is yours, O Lord, and this is your kingdom. We adore you as being in control of everything. Riches and honor come from you alone, and you are the ruler of all mankind; your hand controls power and might, and it is at your discretion that men are made great and given strength.*

❊ ❊ ❊

Be Changed in My Presence

> *Matthew 27:51 (TLB) And look! The curtain secluding the Holiest Place in the Temple was split apart from top to bottom; and the earth shook, and rocks broke,*

Beloved, I removed the separations between us. I've granted you access and encouraged you to come boldly and expectantly. I want time with you face to face. I want My glory to reflect on your countenance. I want you to spend time in My presence, not asking for anything or feeling the need to do anything, just simply being. Being together. Being quiet. Being one.

Come and be changed in My presence. Come and be moved. Let Me love you and teach you how to love like Me - to simply be more like Me: holy. And hear the angels surrounding My throne crying "Holy! Holy! Holy!" Be immersed in Me. Let the atmosphere of heaven penetrate your soul. Be forever changed in My presence and made whole.

❊ ❊ ❊

Prosper and Mature

> *Psalm 1:3 And he will be like a tree firmly planted [and fed] by streams of water, Which yields its fruit in its season; Its leaf does not wither; And in whatever he does, he prospers [and comes to maturity].*

Beloved, be firmly rooted in My Spirit. Yield to His leading and flow. The Spirit can teach you all things; He will not lead you astray. He will refresh and restore you, guide and grow you, and instruct you and give you insight. Under His tutelage, you will prosper and bear fruit, bearing it abundantly as you flourish. Yield to the Spirit, beloved. Trust Our heart for you.

> *John 14:26 (NIV) But the Advocate, the Holy Spirit, whom the Father will send in my name, will teach you all things and will remind you of everything I have said to you.*

> *John 7:39 (NLT) When he said "living water," he was speaking of the Spirit, who would be given to everyone believing in him. But the Spirit had not yet been given, because Jesus had not yet entered into his glory.*

❊ ❊ ❊

Bring Forth Joy

> *Galatians 5:22 (AMP) But the fruit of the Spirit [the result of His presence within us] is...joy,*

Beloved, let joy spring from deep within you like waters bubbling up from the deep. Joy is not dependent on circumstances (happenings) as happiness is, but rather comes from hearts rooted in Me, watered by My Spirit - hearts that know the love of their Creator and the grace they've been extended.

Allow joy to be your perfume, exuding from you as people bask in your presence. May it reflect the difference in you and cause others to see Me in you – to recognize Me in your countenance. Rest in that joy, and hold to it in all circumstances, remembering the joy that comes from Me brings strength. So be strengthened and strengthen others by carrying My joy because it is contagious. Let joy arise!

> *Nehemiah 8:10 (ESV) ...the joy of the Lord is your strength."*

❊ ❊ ❊

Love Well

> *Romans 12:9 (VOICE) Love others well, and don't hide behind a mask; love authentically. Despise evil; pursue what is good as if your life depends on it.*

Beloved, resist the urge to hide who you are, for you have been fearfully and wonderfully made, and you are worth knowing. The real you. Be genuine. Do not fear rejection or concern yourself with those who may misunderstand you. They reject and misunderstand Me as well. I know you and I accept you. May that be sufficient. May My love be sufficient. And may you reflect that love, loving as if you'll never get hurt, trusting that when you do I will heal your heart and comfort you.

Hate that which I hate: evil. The works of the enemy. Not people, beloved, but their unrighteous actions and sin. Love the people. Reflect My heart of grace, righteousness, and mercy. Pursue that which is good and upright. Lead by example. Let your actions speak volumes, and allow your tongue to rest. Love well.

※ ※ ※

Love Takes Action

> *James 1:22 (VOICE) Put the word into action. If you think hearing is what matters most, you are going to find you have been deceived.*

Beloved, knowing My word is vital. You know this to be true. And knowing it is useless without putting it into action. Knowledge puffs up. Love takes action. Love chooses to obey and trust. Love chooses to extend mercy and forgiveness. Love seeks to bless and care for others. Love is reflecting Me.

The enemy will always seek to distort My will. He will twist My word and try to bring confusion. Rely on My Spirit to guide and direct and to bring clarity and discernment. Do not expect perfection because even I don't expect it from you. Be quick to correct your course if you find you've stepped off My path. Repent and realign with Me. I AM patient and slow to anger, and I extend much grace. Receive it and walk well with Me.

> *1 Corinthians 8:1 (AMP) ...Knowledge [alone] makes [people self-righteously] arrogant, but love [that unselfishly seeks the best for others] builds up and encourages others to grow [in wisdom].*

※ ※ ※

Bring Hope

> *John 3:17 (TLB) God did not send his Son into the world to condemn it, but to save it.*

Beloved, too often My children rejoice in judgment, self-congratulating as they take note of the areas they have "right" and highlighting the struggles and sins of others. That does not reflect My heart. I cannot rejoice at progress made in My child's life if it's intentionally contrasted to the downfalls of another. My desire is that not one might be lost.

Find ways to rejoice in your victories without comparison, for comparison isn't how I measure. This is a good thing, for all have sinned and fallen short but One.

So be intentional to bring hope. Say "because I have done this you can too!" Offer encouragement, prayer, and gentle counsel when it is sought. Love like Me. Be known for the love you exude. Shower those around you with hope. Believe the best. See the best. Encourage. Reflect My heart.

❊ ❊ ❊

Hold Fast to the Vision

> *Zechariah 4:10 (TLB) Do not despise this small beginning, for the eyes of the Lord rejoice to see the work begin...*

Beloved, hold fast to the vision I have placed in your heart for it will come to pass and is in fact already here and breaking forth. See the tiny sprouts of green? That is new life bursting forth – a small beginning. Beloved, guard and protect these tender shoots and all they represent, for the enemy of your soul would love to steal, kill, or destroy it; but as you nurture and water it, it will flourish and come to its full fruition.

Resist the urge to be frustrated or impatient at the time required in growing. Remember the journey is needed preparation for what lies ahead. Stay the course. Rejoice in each victory and success no matter how small. Expectantly await the fulfillment of My promises, for they will not return void. Hold fast to the vision, for it will come to pass.

> *Habakkuk 2:2-3 (The Message) And then God answered: "Write this. Write what you see. Write it out in big block letters so that it can be read on the run. This vision-message is a witness pointing to what's coming. It aches for the coming—it can hardly wait! And it doesn't lie. If it seems slow in coming, wait. It's on its way. It will come right on time.*

❈ ❈ ❈

A Hearing Heart of Wisdom and Humility

> *1 Kings 3:9 (JUB) Give, therefore, thy slave a hearing heart to judge thy people that I may discern between good and evil, for who is able to govern this thy so great a people?*

Beloved, like Solomon, desire wisdom. Wisdom to know Me more and to better understand My will and My ways. Wisdom to have a hearing heart – one that knows well My voice. Wisdom to see the ploys of the enemy and be able to thwart them and (when asked) counsel others on how to do the same. Beloved, wisdom is a precious jewel, more valuable than silver and gold. Seek it – seek Me.

With wisdom must come humility. Remember the Source of your wisdom and it will be easier to resist the temptation to get puffed up. In humility and wisdom, walk in My ways and share My truths. Be light and salt, by your very life challenging those around you to reject compromise and seek Me with their whole hearts. So ask Me for wisdom, beloved. It will not be denied.

❊ ❊ ❊

Faithful to the Generations

> *Psalm 103:17 (VOICE) But the unfailing love of the Eternal is always and eternal for those who reverently run after Him. He extends His justice on and on to future generations,*

Beloved, pursue Me. Fix your eyes and stay on course. My love for you never stops. It knows no bounds. I AM a God of justice. I make wrong things right. I extend mercy to those who love Me and to their children and their children's children. I AM faithful.

Pursue Me wholeheartedly. Never losing focus or being taken off track. Run the race victoriously, trusting that your Prize is well worth the effort. For I AM. I AM worth the effort. I AM worth the pursuit. I AM worthy. Period. Love Me because I first loved you.

❊ ❊ ❊

Essential Faithfulness and Truth

> *Psalm 89:8 (AMPC) O Lord God of hosts, who is a mighty one like unto You, O Lord? And Your faithfulness is round about You [an essential part of You at all times].*

Beloved, My faithfulness surrounds Me. It is evident in everything I do and everything I AM. Those who know Me (truly know Me) know I AM faithful, always mindful of My word – watching over it to be certain it comes to pass. I speak only truth for I AM truth. My promises are affirmed – a certainty – bringing forth a resounding "Amen" (So be it)! Thus My character is unimpeachable, sterling, true.

So let your yes be yes and your no be no. Reflect My character, walking in your own faith and faithfulness. May your mouth speak only truth, and may your heart reflect on that which is good and faithful. Be like Me, for you are made in My image. May your integrity be an essential part of who you are and how you are known, that you may be more like Me thus bringing Me glory.

> *2 Corinthians 1:20 (AMPC) For as many as are the promises of God, they all find their Yes in Him [Christ]. For this reason we also utter the Amen (so be it) to God through Him [in His Person and by His agency] to the glory of God.*

* * *

Resting in Perfect and Constant Peace

> *Isaiah 26:3 (AMP) "You will keep in perfect and constant peace the one whose mind is steadfast [that is, committed and focused on You—in both inclination and character], Because he trusts and takes refuge in You [with hope and confident expectation].*

Beloved, quiet your mind and stay focused on Me. Don't allow the distractions of the world to bring fear or chaos. Your inheritance is one of perfect and constant peace. Settle in to Me – like easing into a comfy chair and wrapping yourself up in a warm blanket. Rest in the safety of My love. Be committed and focused on the love and joy that comes from Me. I AM with you always.

Take refuge here in Me. Rest in hope and confident expectation, knowing that I AM by your side, My heavenly hosts fight on your behalf, and nothing can keep Me from loving you. So trust in Me, and know that I AM God.

❊ ❊ ❊

No Portion, Right, or Memorial

> *Nehemiah 2:20 (GW) "The God of heaven will give us success," I answered them. "We, his servants, are going to rebuild. You have no property or claim or historic right in Jerusalem."*

Beloved, I AM the God of heaven. Success comes from My hand. Trust Me to bless and prosper you as you walk in My will and are obedient to My direction. Resist the urge to be distracted or derailed by those claiming to want to help. Be sensitive to My Spirit that I may give you discernment.

The enemy is a trespasser. He will always try to take new territory. Hold fast your boundaries. Say "thus far and no farther." Enforce his lack of claim. Insist on his lack of rights. When it comes to you and that which is yours, you are Mine; therefore, he has no portion, right, or memorial. You are Mine.

❊ ❊ ❊

Time to Flourish and Bloom

> *Isaiah 35:1 (TLB) Even the wilderness and desert will rejoice in those days; the desert will blossom with flowers.*

Beloved, now is the time to bloom! Walk forward in peace and wisdom for it is time to prosper and flourish. My call is given without repentance. I haven't changed My mind about you or the plans I have for you. I will see them through to their completion, never leaving your side, ever cheering you on as you blossom into the fullness of all I've created you for and called you to.

I'm not done with you yet. I have so much more in store. Hang on. Things are not dry or dying, but simply making way for new life. This desert is going to bloom. So make ready and prepare a place, for abundance is about to overtake you – so much that your storehouses won't be able to contain it all. Make ready, beloved. It's time to flourish and bloom!

※ ※ ※

My Rhythm and Harmony

> *Ecclesiastes 3:1 (VOICE) For everything that happens in life—there is a season, a right time for everything under heaven*

Beloved, everything I do has a rhythm and a flow. Each thing in its perfect timing. When an orchestra is playing a powerful piece of music, each instrument, each melody, each beat needs to be in perfect timing - flawlessly synchronized - to create the desired harmony. In the same way, creation is orchestrated for My glory. All are blessed and moved by the way things align, like shivers from a sweeping arpeggio or a grand crescendo.

Each season, each moment perfectly timed. Yield to My flow. Trust My rhythm. I AM always on time: never early, never late. Move with Me – not trying to rush ahead, nor trying to drag your feet. Experience the exquisiteness of My harmony.

※ ※ ※

A Conduit of My Spirit

> *Acts 2:3 (AMP) There appeared to them tongues resembling fire, which were being distributed [among them], and they rested on each one of them [as each person received the Holy Spirit].*

Beloved, let the flame of My Spirit ignite your life and your walk. Operate in the heat of My love, and warm those around by radiating it outward. You are a conduit of Me – of My Spirit – and you are surrounded by people who are in desperate need of a touch from heaven. Be My hands, beloved, and be My touch in the lives around you.

Be ready for divine appointments. Be ready for Me to interrupt your schedule with My agenda. Be ready in season and out. Be ready, beloved. Be ready.

❉ ❉ ❉

Win Them Without a Word

> *Ephesians 6:13, 15 (AMP) Therefore, put on the complete armor of God… and having strapped on your feet the gospel of peace in preparation [to face the enemy with firm-footed stability and the readiness produced by the good news].*

Beloved, share My word. Speak My truth. Speak it in actions birthed from obedience and love. More are watching you than you realize, so never forget Who you host, and let the light, joy, peace, and love of My Spirit pour out from within you. Snatch others from the grip of the enemy with My strong love.

For it is a gospel of peace; that peace that surpasses all understanding that is your inheritance. Cultivate it. Cherish it. Refuse to allow the enemy to steal it. Let it surround you so that as you step close to others, they feel it and want it for themselves. You will win them without a word, beloved, simply through the peace and love in your presence that come from Me.

❊ ❊ ❊

My Crowning Glory

> *Isaiah 62:3 (VOICE) And you will be the crowning glory of the Eternal's power, a royal crown cradled in His palm and held aloft by your God for all to see.*

Beloved, you are My crowning joy, a sparkling gem, My delight, the apple of My eye. My glory is made manifest in you and in your life. I display you for all to see, exalting you that those around you might see Me.

So shine brightly, beloved. It is not arrogance to live to the fullest of what I've created you to be. It is honoring to your Creator. Do not be shamed into diminishing yourself into a muted version of you simply because others are jealous, intimidated, or judgmental. You are My joy and glory. Live to please Me.

❊ ❊ ❊

Cultivate the Peace of My Presence

> *Galatians 5:22 (AMP) But the fruit of the Spirit [the result of His presence within us] is...[inner] peace...*

Beloved, the quiet that you find inside is from Me. Seek it. Cultivate it. Cultivate the quiet that exudes – that shalom that others can feel. It is a tangible and comforting presence, like a deep exhale – rest for the tired and soul-weary. My peace isn't a passive presence. It wars against chaos. As light dispels darkness, My peace dispels chaos and stress.

So find that place within you where I reside. Cultivate and enlarge its footprint in your life. Make room. Make way. Open the doors for Me to flood you with the peace of My presence. Then dwell there, refusing to be moved regardless of circumstances or the world around you. I AM peace and I AM with you. Watch and pray.

※ ※ ※

Godly Patience, a Tangible Love

> *Galatians 5:22 (AMP) But the fruit of the Spirit [the result of His presence within us] is...patience [not the ability to wait, but how we act while waiting]...*

Beloved, remember that your actions reflect on Me. Whether you are aware or not, people watch to see how you react and respond to people and situations.

They want to know if your relationship with Me and My presence within you really make a difference. Pause and ponder what messages you send about Me and whether they're the ones you want and intend to send.

I've instructed you to bear with one another in love. Just as I AM patient and long-suffering with you, I have asked you to do likewise with those around you. Reflect Me. Reflect My heart. Show that the fruit of My Spirit in you is a godly patience that operates in true, tangible love. Let that fruit be manifest for all to see, for it is good.

> *Ephesians 4:2 (GW) Be humble and gentle in every way. Be patient with each other and lovingly accept each other.*

❅ ❅ ❅

Be My Love with Skin On

Note: in scripture, things were often repeated for emphasis in the same way we bold or italicize things now. So when God chooses to repeat something, He's saying, "This is important." With that said, I smiled when He launched into a second day on this scripture. :)

> *Galatians 5:22 (AMP) But the fruit of the Spirit [the result of His presence within us] is…patience [not the ability to wait, but how we act while waiting]…*

Beloved, it is never worth wounding someone's heart for the sake of your schedule, your "rights", or your pride. No matter how pressed for time you may feel, the people I place around you are there by design. They are opportunities to be My love. The frazzled checkout clerk who has been swamped all day may desperately need your smile rather than the curtness of yet another frustrated customer.

You may never know what's going on behind the scenes. You may never know what fruit your actions bring, but I do. I see when your moment of kindness tilts the balance in someone's life so they choose life for one more day rather than giving up. You may not know the full impact your actions have, but that doesn't mean your actions aren't having an impact.

So choose to kill your flesh. Cultivate patience. Respond in love even when the world would say you have a "right" to be affronted. Be My love with skin on. Bear fruit and bear it abundantly.

※ ※ ※

Bridle Your Tongue and Love Like Me

> *James 1:19 (VOICE) Listen, open your ears, harness your desire to speak, and don't get worked up into a rage so easily, my brothers and sisters.*

Beloved, be intentional to bridle your tongue. Resist the urge to vent your frustrations and instead cultivate peace so the frustration won't surface as easily. Like a muscle that can be trained and strengthened, you can increase your ability to hold onto your inner peace. Press into My Spirit. Allow Me to bring you shalom – the peace that wars against chaos – in every circumstance. What you feed will grow. Will you feed the frustration or feed the peace?

Listen, beloved. Hear beyond people's hurts and pride. Hear what is underneath them. Listen with My ears and hear with My heart. See the wounds and brokenness that cause the behavior. Be moved with compassion. Pray for them. Demonstrate My love instead of reacting to offense. Choose to love like Me, and walk in peace and unshakable joy.

> *Proverbs 29:11 (NKJV) A fool vents all his feelings, But a wise man holds them back.*

❊ ❊ ❊

Put Your Confidence in Me

> *Ephesians 6:16 (AMP) Above all, lift up the [protective] shield of faith with which you can extinguish all the flaming arrows of the evil one.*

Beloved, faith is complete confidence in Me. Confidence that I AM who I say I AM. Confidence that I'll do what I've said I'll do. Confidence that I AM. Put your trust in Me for I AM faithful. I AM reliable. I AM trustworthy. I will not let you down. Rest in Me.

Let your faith be unshakable. Let no circumstance or situation give you pause to wonder about Me. I AM always at work and always working for the good. Let your faith in Me be unshakable. Shadrach, Meshach, and Abed-nego said to Nebuchadnezzar, "our God is able to rescue us... but even if He doesn't we will serve no other." Their faith in Me and My plans was steadfast. In the same way beloved, let your faith surpass your ability to understand what I am doing and simply trust. I AM worthy of your faith for I AM El Aman, the Faithful God.

> *Daniel 3:16-18 (VOICE) Shadrach, Meshach, and Abed-nego: Nebuchadnezzar, we have no need to defend our actions in this matter. We are ready for the test. If you throw us into the blazing furnace, then the God we serve is able to rescue us from a furnace of blazing fire and release us from your power, Your Majesty. But even if He does not, O king, you can be sure that we still will not serve your gods and we will not worship the golden statue you erected.*

❈ ❈ ❈

I AM God Most Able (Elohim Yakol)

> *Matthew 19:26 (NLT) Jesus looked at them intently and said, "Humanly speaking, it is impossible. But with God everything is possible."*

Beloved, nothing is too hard for Me. I AM able to see the way through every situation. Nothing shocks or overwhelms me. I AM the God who is able, Elohim Yakol (God Most Able). You can rely on Me. I AM trustworthy and worthy of your faith. Nothing is impossible for Me.

I love to show My fingerprints – to do things to build your confidence, to wait and see whether you'll notice My hand at work and what your response will be. Will you thank Me? Will you give glory and honor? Will you testify of My goodness? Just as you like to be encouraged, I do too. You are made in My image. I like when you love on Me and encourage Me. Love as you want to be loved.

❉ ❉ ❉

Refuse to Be Dimmed

> *Ephesians 5:4 (GW) It's not right that dirty stories, foolish talk, or obscene jokes should be mentioned among you either. Instead, give thanks to God.*

Beloved, you are in the world, but not of it. Let your words and actions demonstrate what a difference it makes to be filled with Me. Stay mindful of what is pleasing and honoring to Me – as well as what isn't – and choose wisely. Resist the temptation to feel pressured into compromise simply because of who else does and how many do.

You are light. Refuse to allow that light to be tainted or dimmed, but rather shine brightly, forcing the darkness to scurry away. And by darkness, beloved, I do not mean the people, but rather the spirits in operation behind the people's words and actions. Never forget there is a difference. And we love the people, even (and especially) when we can clearly see the enemy's hand at play. Often that is when they need it most.

❊ ❊ ❊

Stand Fast

> *2 Corinthians 10:5 (AMP) We are destroying sophisticated arguments and every exalted and proud thing that sets itself up against the [true] knowledge of God, and we are taking every thought and purpose captive to the obedience of Christ,*

Beloved, stand fast. You know Me. When someone tells lies about you to your loved ones, what response do you desire them to have? Would you have them tuck tail and buy into the lies or stand fast and refuse to be moved - to know you so well that nothing can shake what they know to be true?

Beloved, that is what I desire, too: for My children to know Me so well that they won't attack My character when the lies and whispers of the enemy come, but rather let their vision of who I AM be immovable. Firmly rooted in the Truth. Unshakable. So that no lie can distort, no circumstance discourage. So that you all might know who I AM - that I AM good. That I AM for you and not against you. That I AM righteous and merciful. That I AM love. And that you are Mine.

❊ ❊ ❊

Pursue Me

> *Psalm 84:10 (NIV) Better is one day in your courts than a thousand elsewhere; I would rather be a doorkeeper in the house of my God than dwell in the tents of the wicked.*

Beloved, there is no place so sweet as My presence. I AM worth the time – worth the effort. The rest and refreshing that comes in My presence is deep and cleansing. Fight through the noise around you to find that quiet place of peace. I AM there. I AM waiting. I AM always with you.

Be hungry and thirsty for Me beloved. Be insatiable. I AM worth the effort. Just to know Me is worth it, not to mention the blessings that pour forth from time with Me. I AM worth your pursuit. Find the time. Refuse to allow distractions to keep you from being with Me. I AM like air to you – necessary for life - for I AM life. I AM the life-giver. I AM the healer. I AM the refresher. I AM the Lover of Your Soul. Pursue Me.

> *Matthew 5:6 (GW) Blessed are those who hunger and thirst for God's approval. They will be satisfied.*

※ ※ ※

I AM YHVH Ezer (the Lord your helper)

> *Psalm 118:13 (TLB) You did your best to kill me, O my enemy, but the Lord helped me.*

Beloved, know I AM with you always. I AM YHVH Ezer, the Lord your helper. Though the enemy may relentlessly seek to kill, steal, and destroy, I WILL NOT leave you. I will fight for you and by your side. I have given My angels charge over you to keep and protect you. I will snatch your feet from the net. The traps the enemy has laid for you WILL NOT succeed.

Lift up your eyes, beloved. Your help comes from Me. Never lose sight of Me. Keep your gaze fixed steadfastly. The storms may rage, but let nothing steal your attention for I AM greater than any storm or trial. Nothing is to strong for Me. For I AM YHVH. I AM the Lord.

> *Psalm 33:20 (ASV) Our soul hath waited for Jehovah: He is our help and our shield.*
>
> *Psalm 25:15 (ESV) My eyes are ever toward the Lord, for he will pluck my feet out of the net.*
>
> *Psalm 121:1-2 (ESV) I lift up my eyes to the hills. From where does my help come? My help comes from the Lord, who made heaven and earth.*

❉ ❉ ❉

Cling and Sing

> *Psalm 118:14 (VOICE) He is my strength, and He is the reason I sing; He has been there to save me in every situation.*

Beloved, praise Me in every situation. I AM your strength. I AM El Maowz (God your strength). Allow Me to strengthen you, beloved, regardless of circumstances. Praise Me. Let joy pour forth from deep in your soul because I AM worthy. Let your songs of love be a victory cry. Refuse to waver. Trust Me implicitly.

I AM Yeshua (your salvation). My hand is extended to you, beloved. Take hold. Cling to Me. I AM strong and I will strengthen. We will stand fast together. The enemy cannot stand against us, so cling and sing. Cling and sing, beloved. Your deliverance is here.

> *2 Samuel 22:33 (NKJV) God [is] my strength [and] power, And He makes my way perfect.*

* * *

Let Your Cry of Victory Ring

> *Psalm 118:16 (VOICE) The mighty arm of the Eternal is raised in victory; the right hand of His has shown His power."*

Beloved, raise a shout of victory! We shall not be defeated. Sound a cry in declaration that we are victorious. Raise your voice! Do not be afraid that you will be put to shame. Lean on Me. Trust in Me. I AM the God of heaven (El Shamayim) and earth, the Lord of Hosts (YHVH Sabaoth), the King of Glory (Melek Kabowd). Nothing is too hard for Me!

Rightly understand Who I AM and what I AM capable of. I AM the God who parted the sea, brought forth water from a rock, and sent manna from heaven. I make a way where there seems to be no way. Don't focus on possible solutions YOU see in a situation, for I see things you do not. So simply focus on Me, on who I AM, and let your victory cry ring!

* * *

Beloved {Moments with God}

Sitting in His presence quietly waiting to hear His voice. I hear the whisper, "Beloved." I know that's just the beginning of what He plans to say, and yet I get stuck there, feeling my throat begin to tighten and tears begin to well as I ponder the privilege it is for Him to call us – call me – by that name.

I am His beloved and He is mine. I know this intellectually, but most days what that actually means barely penetrates the surface. I am My beloved's and My Beloved is mine. I hear Him whisper, "Yes. Yes, My love." I know He's encouraging me to let this sink in deeper, to let it be more than simply a saying written in Hebrew on a ring that never leaves my hand. To know. To truly know.

"Papa, why is it that so many of us struggle so much to simply receive the love You're pouring out to us?"

I hear His gentle reply, "The enemy has been holding a broken mirror in front of your faces for so long that one that is whole feels false. Your minds have calibrated the distortion as truth. It throws everything else out of alignment because it is all based on a lie."

"Papa help us to recalibrate. Help us to align with You, to align with Truth."

And as though I can feel His warm breath carrying the gentle "yes" and His arms surrounding me, Olam Zeroa, the Everlasting Arms, is gripping me tightly, refusing to give up on me regardless of how broken or messy I feel. He is always there. He always is loving me. Truly I AM "beloved."

> *Song of Solomon 6:3 (AMP) I am my beloved's and my beloved is mine…*

❊ ❊ ❊

Operate in Love and Be Unoffendable

> *Philippians 1:9 (TLV) Now this I pray, that your love might overflow still more and more in knowledge and depth of discernment,*

Beloved, as you operate in love, I will open your eyes and show you things you otherwise wouldn't see. There are things you can only discern when you're filtering through a loving gaze. Operate in love and be unoffendable. Extend much grace. Be rich in mercy. Stifle pride and your "right" to respond in a particular way, and instead be like Me.

Refuse to be the wicked servant, holding a debt over someone's head that you yourself have been forgiven. Be like Me. Respond like Me. Be patient and long-suffering. Let your love continually increase. Let your heart grow more and more like Mine. Let My love be shed abroad in your heart and may it increase your discernment exponentially.

> *Romans 5:5 (KJV) And hope maketh not ashamed; because the love of God is shed abroad in our hearts by the Holy Ghost which is given unto us.*

❈ ❈ ❈

Hear Me Even in Your Sleep

> *Job 33:15-16 (AMP) In a dream, a vision of the night [one may hear God's voice], When deep sleep falls on men While slumbering upon the bed, Then He opens the ears of men And seals their instruction,*

Beloved, hear My whispers as you sleep. Recognize My heart. Know My voice. Feel My touch. Receive My wisdom. Heed My warnings. Feel My hand upon you as I seal My instruction in your heart. Yield to My direction. Hold fast when you awaken. Refuse to allow My download to be stolen or dismissed.

I have opened the ears of your heart. You can hear Me, beloved. Choose to be open and rest. Choose to listen. I AM moving as you sleep. I never slumber; I never sleep. I AM always aware of you and the things pertaining to you. So rest in Me, knowing I AM covering you. Healing and speaking. Protecting and refreshing.

Open your heart to hear My voice as your flesh is silent and your natural mind is not spinning or fighting My words with your own sense of logic or understanding. Hear Me, beloved. Receive, understand, and yield.

> *Psalm 121:3-4 (TLB) He will never let me stumble, slip, or fall. For he is always watching, never sleeping.*

❊ ❊ ❊

Take the Limits Off Your Expectations of Me

> *Isaiah 45:3 (JUB) And I will give thee the hidden treasures and the well-guarded secrets that thou may know that I am the LORD, the God of Israel, who gives thee thy name.*

Beloved, nothing is hidden from Me. I haven't lost anything nor will I ever struggle to put something in your hand. I AM sovereign. Be a yielded vessel and truly surrender all you have to Me that I may position you and equip you as I desire. Hold Me and relationship with Me dearest of all.

I will whisper to you secret things you have not known. I will supernaturally provide for you. I will move in and through you in ways you cannot imagine. See with My eyes and hear with My heart. Know that each soul is more valuable to Me than any amount of silver. Discern true worth and refuse to be sucked in by the world's system. Allow Me to move. Take the limits off your expectations of Me and give Me room to perform.

❊ ❊ ❊

Let Love Supersede All

> *Matthew 18:13-14 (GW) I can guarantee this truth: If he finds it, he is happier about it than about the 99 that have not strayed. In the same way, your Father in heaven does not want one of these little ones to be lost.*

Beloved, I desire that not one would be lost. I AM not angry at those who have wandered away. I only long for their return. Will you walk in love and accurately reflect My heart so that My beloveds know I ache for them? Will you withhold judgment, instead extending mercy and understanding? Will you resist the urge to indulge in self-righteousness and pride and instead be humble, long-suffering, compassionate, and full of grace? You are made in My image, reflect Me accurately.

Refuse to be the prodigal's older brother – resentful of the Father's love for the one who'd gone astray. Love in no way excuses sin; it simply says the person and their heart is more important. Be known by your love. Draw others home by your love. Let love change them. Let love change you. Let love supersede all.

❊ ❊ ❊

Accurately Reflect Me

> *Luke 17:1-3 (GW) ...how horrible it will be for the person who causes someone to lose his faith! It would be best for that person to be thrown into the sea with a large stone hung around his neck than for him to cause one of these little ones to lose his faith. So watch yourselves!...*

Beloved, be mindful of your actions and how they affect others. Yes, you each have personal responsibility for your choices, but you do not want to be the one to cause someone to stumble or fall away just as you don't want someone to cause you to stumble or fall away.

Therefore it is vital you be like Me. Love like Me. Accurately reflect Me. This cannot be stressed enough. I see the full impact of careless words and thoughtless actions, and if you could fully grasp the effect they have, you would feel the weight of them. They are not to be taken lightly.

My Word is there to instruct you in how to live. Beloved, eat it as though you were a starving man. It is good and nourishing to your soul. It brings forth life and teaches you to be like Me. So immerse yourself. Be saturated by the water of My word that you might pour out that living water in a dry and thirsty land.

※ ※ ※

Yield to My Sanctification

> *John 17:17 (AMP) Sanctify them in the truth [set them apart for Your purposes, make them holy]; Your word is truth.*

Beloved, allow yourself to decrease that I might increase within you. Yield to My refining process. Let Me burn away the dross, leaving you brilliant and sparkling that you may shine blindingly brightly. This is My sanctifying process: the process by which you become more like Me – more radiant – that your countenance might glow from My glory. Waves of glory!

I have new levels for you. I AM shifting the atmosphere and opening up heaven to draw you in closer still to Me. Allow Me to gently change you into the fullness of all I've called you to be. Give the process the time it needs. The journey itself is a blessing, and rushing the process only causes you to miss points along the way, so yield to both My process and My pace. I will increase My blessings upon you. Receive, beloved.

> *John 3:30 (NKJV) He must increase, but I must decrease.*

❊ ❊ ❊

Greater is the Light Within You

> *John 1:5 (AMPC) And the Light shines on in the darkness, for the darkness has never overpowered it*

[put it out or absorbed it or appropriated it, and is unreceptive to it].

Beloved, darkness cannot resist the light. It must surrender to it. I AM light. Everything is darkness compared to the light of My glory. But you, beloved, made in My image, are a carrier of My presence – My glory; therefore you also shine brightly, drawing those in darkness to the brilliance of your glow.

Do not be afraid of the darkness, for far greater is the Light within you. You have nothing to fear. The darkness merely highlights the splendor of your radiance. Christ in you, the hope of glory. Joy and salvation. Shine brightly and unashamedly. Like a prism bursting forth into beaming rays of opalescent light, so My children burst forth in facets of My beauty – glorious and splendid, a feast for My heart.

※ ※ ※

My Light Prevails

Psalm 18:11-12 (TPT) Wrapped and hidden in the thick-cloud darkness His thunder-tabernacle surrounding Him. He hid Himself in mystery-darkness, the dense rain clouds were His garments. Suddenly, the brilliance of His presence breaks through...

Beloved, in the shadow of the Almighty – My shadow – you are safe, protected, restored, recharged, prepared, transformed, and made whole. My brilliance breaks through both from Me directly and from you as one who carries My presence. It is a deep warfare – light chasing the darkness – and not even chasing, dispelling. Almost like no fight is necessary, but simply to "be." Simply to shine.

I bring beauty even in your night seasons and reveal the mysteries of heaven in the hidden places. I AM the Revealer of Mysteries – Gelah Raz – the Holy One of Israel. Make Me your dwelling place, your shelter in the storm, because even when the storm rages, My light prevails.

※ ※ ※

Firmly Rooted in Me

> *John 15:5 (VOICE) I am the vine, and you are the branches. If you abide in Me and I in you, you will bear great fruit. Without Me, you will accomplish nothing.*

Beloved, stay rooted in Me. Abide in Me. Rest, tarry, remain… BE with Me. Then watch. Watch the fruit pour forth from your life – so much you can't contain it. So much it cannot be ignored or denied. My hand of blessing evident on your life.

Resist the urge to cut yourself off from My life-giving flow. Like a flower cut and placed on display, the appearance of life will linger for a season, but when you are cut off from life, you are dying – even if it isn't immediately evident. Distractions will always be around you, vying for your attention, but cultivate steady focus. Be firmly rooted in Me.

※ ※ ※

Ripe With Possibility

> *Song of Solomon 2:13 (TLB) The leaves are coming out, and the grapevines are in blossom. How delicious they smell! Arise, my love, my fair one, and come away.'*

Beloved, the time is ripe and the harvest season upon us. Open the doors of the storehouses, and prepare to fill them with the choicest fruits.

Awaken your senses! Be aware of all the possibilities around you. The moment is ripe with possibility. Be alert. Tune in. Align with My frequency and wait on Me. The time is now. Break forth. Burst forth. As you have sown, you shall receive.

※ ※ ※

Able and Willing

> *Psalm 40:5 (CJB) How much you have done, Adonai my God! Your wonders and your thoughts toward us — none can compare with you! I would proclaim them, I would speak about them; but there's too much to tell!*

Beloved, I AM the God of Wonders. Pause and behold My handiwork. See Me for who I AM. Do not allow doubt or circumstances to minimize Me in your eyes. Nothing is too hard for Me. And I love you. You are My beloved, My heart, the apple of My eye, and the center of My world.

Do you think that I could part the seas, but somehow be incapable of moving on your behalf? Or perhaps you think Me able but unwilling? Don't fall prey to those lies. Trust Me. Trust My plans for you, and yield to Me. Look with wonder upon My glory. Watch Me in action. Refuse to be moved or shaken. Know that I AM God.

※ ※ ※

See Yourself Rightly

> *Romans 12:3 (CJB) For I am telling every single one of you, through the grace that has been given to me, not to have exaggerated ideas about your own importance. Instead, develop a sober estimate of yourself based on the standard which God has given to each of you, namely, trust.*

Beloved, refuse to let pride have any hold on your life or let false humility take root. Seeing yourself as less than what You were created to be does just as much disservice to Me, your Creator, as allowing yourself to be puffed up. Ask Me for an accurate understanding of who you are. Then when I tell you, believe Me. Allow Me to mold your understanding of yourself – what you're capable of, who you've been created to be, how I see you, and who you truly are.

You have been fearfully and wonderfully made. Allowing yourself to believe that and using to its fullest that which you've been given honors Me. So resist the urge to hold back whether you're tempted to do so because you fear failure, or because others are intimidated by the greatness in you, or for any reason in between. Think only of pleasing Me, beloved. The thoughts and concerns of man should not hold more weight than Me. Trust Me. Trust My judgment in how I have created you and called you. See yourself rightly and be all I have made you to be.

❊ ❊ ❊

I AM Willing Because You Are Worth It

> *Psalm 136:1 (VOICE) Let your heart overflow with praise to the Eternal, for He is good, for His faithful love lasts forever.*

Beloved, I AM good. My heart towards you is good. I AM unchanging, ever faithful, steadfast, worthy of your trust. Pause and reflect on that. Pause and consider if you truly believe that My heart towards you is good, or if you just pay lip service to those sentiments you know you're supposed to have.

I desire real relationship with you. I desire authenticity. Yes, I want you to trust Me, and yes, I'm worthy of that trust, but I want it to be freely given – not out of a sense of obligation, but from a heart overflowing with love for Me. If that isn't where you are yet beloved, I'm not angry about that. I'm willing to put in the time and work to show you who I AM. Are you willing to take the time and open your heart to see Me as I AM?

※ ※ ※

Lead by Example and Pray

> *Proverbs 14:34 (VOICE) Living according to God's instructions makes a nation great, but sin colors those who commit it with disgrace.*

Beloved, lead by example. Walk in freedom unhindered by sinful pursuits. Keep your mind – thoughts and actions – fixed on Me. Operate in love rather than being tempted to pride or judgment. Encourage others to be their best selves by being your best self. Show them what it looks like. Let them ask you how to walk that way rather then judging their ungodly behavior as they are still in the world.

Pray for them. Pray for your nation. Pray for your leaders. I AM sovereign. I lift men up and make them great. Trust that My will can be accomplished on earth and pray that it will be. Ultimately you are in My hands, and that is a good place to be.

> *1 Chronicles 29:11-12 (NLT) Yours, O Lord, is the greatness, the power, the glory, the victory, and the majesty. Everything in the heavens and on earth is*

yours, O Lord, and this is your kingdom. We adore you as the one who is over all things. Wealth and honor come from you alone, for you rule over everything. Power and might are in your hand, and at your discretion people are made great and given strength.

❊ ❊ ❊

I AM Who I AM and I AM Unchanging

Revelation 19:11 (AMPC) After that I saw heaven opened, and behold, a white horse [appeared]! The One Who was riding it is called Faithful (Trustworthy, Loyal, Incorruptible, Steady) and True, and He passes judgment and wages war in righteousness (holiness, justice, and uprightness).

Beloved, I AM faithful. I AM true. I AM fiercely loyal and perfectly steadfast. I can be fully trusted, and I AM incapable of being corrupted or influenced to change My character. I AM who I AM and I AM unchanging. You can depend on Me. If I say it, I will do it.

I AM love - rich in mercy, and slow to anger. When I wage war, I do so with integrity in justice. I AM holy. I fight on behalf of the ones I love. I am stirred with righteous anger towards the enemy and his plots and ploys against you. I will not be silent, for I am YHVH Sabaoth (the Lord of Hosts). I will fight for those I love and on their behalf, for they rely on Me. I AM faithful and steadfast, and I AM victorious.

Numbers 23:19 (GW) God is not like people. He tells no lies. He is not like humans. He doesn't change his mind. When he says something, he does it. When he makes a promise, he keeps it.

❅ ❅ ❅

Declare My Greatness

Isaiah 12:4 (VOICE)…Give thanks to the Eternal; call on His name. Spread the news throughout the world of what He has done and how great is His name!

Beloved, I AM worthy. Declare My greatness throughout the earth. Testify. Share all that I have done in and for you. I AM great and greatly to be praised.

Call on My name, for I AM faithful and worthy and mighty, and I love moving on behalf of My children. Keep your heart in an attitude of thanksgiving. Be mindful to see My handiwork, for I love to bless you, just as I love being blessed by you. Hold Me close, beloved. You move My heart.

❅ ❅ ❅

I AM the Life Giver

Psalm 78:20 (VOICE) He split open the rock, and water gushed out; streams and rivers were overflowing!…

Beloved, I AM the Life Giver. Just as the rain saturates the ground causing it to flourish, so I will pour out My life-giving flow of Holy Spirit over you that you might flourish and bring forth life, and bring it more abundantly. I am even now saturating you. Receive!

No heart is too broken or cracked, no heart is too hardened or dead for Me. Have I not brought forth life-giving water from a rock? Nothing is too hard for Me. I will saturate you. I will overflow your spirit with My own. I will bring forth life in the desert places because I AM the giver of life and I love to see you flourish.

※ ※ ※

I AM Burning Away That Which Restrains You

> *Isaiah 43:2 (VOICE) When you face stormy seas I will be there with you with endurance and calm; you will not be engulfed in raging rivers. If it seems like you're walking through fire with flames licking at your limbs, keep going; you won't be burned.*

Beloved, I AM baptizing you with fire - immersing and consuming you. All the dross is being burned away, and your face will shine with a pure radiance that can only come from knowing Me and basking in My glory.

Let My fire wash over you like waves. And as Shadrach, Meshach, and Abed-nego walked among the flames which burned only the ropes holding them in bondage (Daniel 3:25), so shall My flames be over you. I AM igniting you and setting you ablaze for My glory! I AM burning away that which restrains and holds you back. Walk in the fire and do not be burned. Be beautified, glorified, and made new.

❊ ❊ ❊

I AM Your Strong Tower

> *Isaiah 58:8 (VOICE) Then, oh then, your light will break out like the warm, golden rays of a rising sun; in an instant, you will be healed. Your rightness will precede and protect you; the glory of the Eternal will follow and defend you.*

Beloved, as you walk in righteousness, it is My joy to defend you. I will silence the tongues that seek to slander you and bring destruction on those who would seek your ruin. Behold, I AM a Jealous God. I love My people beyond comprehension. Woe to them that would stand against you.

I have given the warning: do not touch My anointed. I have cautioned and made the consequences clear. I protect what is Mine, and beloved, you are Mine. I both cover you with My feathers (gently protecting), and I AM the Lord of Hosts (waging war on your behalf). You are not without covering. I AM your strong tower. You are safe in Me.

> *1 Chronicles 16:22 (AMP) "Do not touch My anointed ones, And do My prophets no harm."*

❊ ❊ ❊

Do Not Fear Temptation

> *Matthew 4:1 (TLB) Then Jesus was led out into the wilderness by the Holy Spirit, to be tempted there by Satan.*

Beloved, do not be afraid of temptation, for I will not give you more than you can handle. I AM with you – beside you – here to strengthen you when you reach for me. I will always provide a means of escape. No trap set by the enemy to ensnare you is without a means of deliverance.

Change your point of view. Embrace each temptation as an opportunity to build strength, your inner fortitude. See each one as an opportunity to find your strength by relying more heavily on Me, that in your weakness My power might be made perfect. My grace is sufficient, beloved. Rest and rely on Me.

> *1 Corinthians 10:13 (GW) There isn't any temptation that you have experienced which is unusual for humans. God, who faithfully keeps his promises, will not allow you to be tempted beyond your power to resist. But when you are tempted, he will also give you the ability to endure the temptation as your way of escape.*
>
> *2 Corinthians 12:9 (ESV) …My grace is sufficient for you, for my power is made perfect in weakness…*

❖ ❖ ❖

Unaware But Not Unappreciative

> *Psalm 91:11 (NET) For he will order his angels to protect you in all you do.*

Beloved, I AM the Lord of heavenly armies. All the hosts of heaven are at My command, and you are My most prized possession – the apple of My eye and core of My heart. You are vital to Me. Therefore I have given My angels charge over you to guard and protect you, and it is their pleasure to carry out My command.

They are ever present, acting on My behalf and for your benefit. Beloved, you will never fully know all the harm that has been averted and minimized because My faithful hosts have shielded you from it. It is understood that you are unaware of all that happens on your behalf, but do not be unappreciative simply because you are unaware. Be slow to accuse Me of negligence, and remember that I desire good for you even more than you do for yourself.

※ ※ ※

Pleased to Serve

> *Psalm 104:4 (VOICE) You make Your messengers like the winds; the breeze whispers Your words, Your servants are like the fire and flame.*

Beloved, My hosts surround you, fulfilling My commands. They carry out each of My instructions with precision and dedication, and it pleases them to do so – to serve the sons of man on My behalf.

They serve Me because they see Me in all My glory and grandeur; they know that I AM God. How awesome and humbling it is for them to see you – who have seen Me as through a glass, darkly – yielded and worshipping Me with whole hearts! Yes, beloved, they are pleased to serve the ones who operate in such faith.

Be aware of their presence. Be aware and know they are an extension of Me.

> *1 Corinthians 13:12 (KJV) For now we see through a glass, darkly; but then face to face: now I know in part; but then shall I know even as also I am known.*

※ ※ ※

I Have Spoken Your Name

> *Psalm 139:23 (VOICE) Explore me, O God, and know the real me. Dig deeply and discover who I am...*

Beloved, I see who you truly are, for I know who you've been created to be because I AM Creator. I know you. I AM calling forth your true self. Just as death couldn't hold Lazarus back when he was called forth, nothing will keep you from walking in all I have called you to, for I have spoken your name.

So walk boldly, beloved. Let nothing hinder or hold you back. My voice is the voice of many waters, and it breaks even the mighty cedars. Surely you know that when I speak chains are broken and no restraint can stand. Be free, beloved! Be free!

> *Psalm 29:5 (NLT) The voice of the Lord splits the mighty cedars; the Lord shatters the cedars of Lebanon.*

❊ ❊ ❊

Choose Holiness

> *Exodus 28:36 (KJV) And thou shalt make a plate of pure gold, and grave upon it, like the engravings of a signet, Holiness To The Lord.*

Beloved, just as I had the high priest wear the engraving "Holiness to the Lord" against his forehead – a frontlet between his eyes – so you must keep your mind's eye fixed on holiness. Choose it. Be intentional about it. Choose it out of love for Me because it is pleasing to Me, and choose it for yourself because it is good for you.

I am Elohim Qadosh, the Holy God. You are made in My image. Walk like Me. I know that even as you try to be holy there will be times you fall short, but beloved, don't allow a lack of perfection to discourage you from even trying. Not being able to perfectly execute something does not absolve you of the responsibility of trying. Choose rightly, beloved. No matter what the world says, choose well. Resist temptation. You are able. I AM with you to strengthen you. Be holy as I AM holy.

> *Leviticus 19:2 (NLT) ...You must be holy because I, the Lord your God, am holy.*

❊ ❊ ❊

Kindness is Contagious

> *Galatians 5:22-23 (AMP) But the fruit of the Spirit [the result of His presence within us] is... kindness,*

Beloved, as My fruit multiplies within you, let it pour forth from your heart in the form of kindness. Be known for being one who is gracious and generous of spirit, full of mercy and overflowing with compassion. Let kindness be your trademark.

Nurture others' wellbeing, making their interests your focus, trusting that I will make yours My own. Encourage those around you to operate in joy and love simply by doing so yourself. Kindness is contagious. Spread it liberally!

❊ ❊ ❊

Sober and Singleminded

> *Proverbs 4:25 (AMPC) Let your eyes look right on [with fixed purpose], and let your gaze be straight before you.*

Beloved, resist the urge to be sidetracked or to lose focus. I have given you purpose and a call, and, behold, it is good and worthy – worthy of your time, attention, and focus. So keep your gaze fixed, not looking to the left or to the right, and not wasting time looking back. For I AM your rear guard, and I go before you. There is nothing to fear.

The cares of this world may try to draw you in through worry and fear, and the temptations of this world will seek to lull you into complacency, but you know – you know, beloved – that time is short. So be sober and singleminded in purpose. Expand the Kingdom and make My name great.

※ ※ ※

Delivered Promises

> *Revelation 21:11 (VOICE) It gleamed and shined with the glory of God; its radiance was like the most precious of jewels, like jasper, and it was as clear as crystal.*

Beloved, what I promise, I deliver. And when it arrives, it is typically bigger, better, and more beautiful than could have been expected. I AM more than enough. Hold to Me. My word is unshakable. If I have said it, it is done. Immovable and unstoppable, My word will always accomplish My will.

I AM more than enough. Be satisfied in Me not in what I can give you, but in Who I AM. I have not forgotten the promises made you. The time for their fruition is nearly upon us. Patience, My love. Trust Me and hold fast.

❊ ❊ ❊

Align, Abide, Bear Fruit

> *John 15:16 (GW) ...I have appointed you to go, to produce fruit that will last, and to ask the Father in my name to give you whatever you ask for.*

Beloved, I have created you to bear fruit – fruit that will last. See with My eyes and hear with My heart. As you do you will know what to ask for and when, and you will know you do so in My name and under My authority. Then watch Me respond.

Be moved with compassion. Hear past the outer layer of a situation to the heart of the matter. Allow your discernment to grow and increase as you cultivate your spiritual senses and tune in more and more accurately to My frequency. Be patient with the process, and remember it will always be ongoing. For you cannot begin to fathom the depths of Me. Allow My Spirit time and space to move in you. Align with Me. Abide in Me. Bear fruit.

❊ ❊ ❊

Breathing Life

> *Genesis 2:7 (GW) Then the Lord God formed the man from the dust of the earth and blew the breath of life into his nostrils. The man became a living being.*

Beloved, My breath brings life. Ask Me to breath into situations and over people. Ask for My breath of life – My Spirit – to change things. Ask Me. Feel My breath, My wind, in your life. I AM moving, beloved. Like a desert suddenly blooming, My breath of life brings dramatic change – refreshing and hope. Embrace it. Welcome and encourage it.

Remember that life is in you, beloved. You live because My breath is in your lungs. Breathe that life out onto others. Be intentional to do it. Choose life. Choose to release it over others. Carefully choose your words, beloved, and select only those that bring life. You are made in My image. Reflect Me.

※ ※ ※

Love Well

> *Ephesians 4:2 (TLB) Be humble and gentle. Be patient with each other, making allowance for each other's faults because of your love.*

Beloved, I AM glorified as you accurately reflect My character and nature – you who were created in My image. As you walk in grace, loving one another well – being patient and kind (never jealous or proud, haughty or unkind, selfish or rude), being mindful to seek others' well-being and promotion above your own, rejoicing in each other's victories and comforting in losses, and ever being loyal and steadfast – beloved, that kind of love honors Me. It demonstrates My character without a word. Those actions testify to My goodness simply by moving in the hearts of those touched by that love.

Actions like that bring Me glory – a glory that radiates in the spiritual realm as fireworks would in the natural. And even those who may not "see" it in the spirit can feel and respond to it – often without even realizing what they are responding to. So continue to love well, beloved, and bring Me glory.

> *1 Corinthians 13:4-8 (TLB) Love is very patient and kind, never jealous or envious, never boastful or proud, never haughty or selfish or rude. Love does not demand its own way. It is not irritable or touchy. It does not hold grudges and will hardly even notice when others do it wrong. It is never glad about injustice, but rejoices whenever truth wins out. If you love someone, you will be loyal to him no matter what the cost. You will always believe in him, always expect the best of him, and always stand your ground in defending him. All the special gifts and powers from God will someday come to an end, but love goes on forever…*

❖ ❖ ❖

Let Your Anticipation Testify

> *Psalm 130:6 (VOICE) My soul waits for the Lord to break into the world more than night watchmen expect the break of day, even more than night watchmen expect the break of day.*

Beloved, be a watchman on the wall. Alertly fix your gaze, watching expectantly for Me to break through, for I AM the God of the breakthrough. Let your heart stand in faith, knowing with full certainty that I will move suddenly. It may seem as though I tarry, but I tarry not.

Anticipate Me. Be sober, alert, and ready – expectant, filled with confidence and trust in Me and My word. May your anticipation alone testify to your faith in who I AM and in My faithfulness.

❊ ❊ ❊

Increase Comes Through Me

> *John 15:4 (GW) Live in me, and I will live in you. A branch cannot produce any fruit by itself. It has to stay attached to the vine. In the same way, you cannot produce fruit unless you live in me.*

Beloved, increase comes from Me. Stay firmly rooted. Life can only come from the source. Draw from Me. Drink deeply from My living water – the flow of My Spirit. Be saturated in My presence, and allow that rich, life-giving atmosphere to bring forth much fruit.

Deep wells pour forth, gurgling up from deep within you as My Spirit stirs and hovers over you as you rest and dwell in My presence. Behold, I AM doing a new thing Will you not know it? *[I sense Him smiling as He asks that as though He knows already that, of COURSE, you will want to know it.]* New life – increase – is coming. Increase is here.

Isaiah 43:19 (VOICE) Watch closely: I am preparing something new; it's happening now, even as I speak, and you're about to see it. I am preparing a way through the desert; Waters will flow where there had been none.

❊ ❊ ❊

I Will Meet You in Your Dreams

Psalm 3:5 (VOICE) I lie down at night and fall asleep. I awake in the morning—healthy, strong, vibrant—because the Eternal supports me.

Beloved, I AM with you always. Rest in Me. As you yield to Me even in your sleep, I will meet you there for times of refreshing and impartation. Be ready to receive. Come with your heart prepared to meet with Me. Truly you cannot begin to imagine all that I want to share with you there, beloved.

Be ready to be commissioned. Be ready to be mantled. Be ready to be radically and completely healed and transformed. Come ready to lower your guard. You don't need it with Me anyway, and your logic won't help you here. My ways are not your ways. Simply trust and yield. Take Me at My word and receive.

❊ ❊ ❊

Fill Yourself with the Unshakable Understanding of Who I AM

> *Revelation 4:2 (TLB) And instantly I was in spirit there in heaven and saw—oh, the glory of it!—a throne and someone sitting on it!*

Beloved, quiet your soul, quiet your spirit. Let Me sweep you away – whether to catch you up into the heavenlies or simply have you rest in My presence. Meet with Me. Be saturated in My glory. Allow yourself to be completely overwhelmed and undone by My presence and the full saturating love you feel from Me.

Fill yourself with the unshakable understanding of Who I AM. For if you fully and truly receive that understanding, you cannot operate in fear because you know the One who loves you is greater and higher by far than any other. Of whom shall you be afraid? I AM on your side. Be overwhelmed by My glory, and walk in the full confidence of one who knows they have nothing to fear.

※ ※ ※

Be a Conduit of Blessing and Grace

> *Psalm 112:5 (VOICE) Good comes to all who are gracious and share freely; they conduct their affairs with sound judgment.*

Beloved, just as I have extended grace to you, you (being made in My image) should be intentional about extending grace to others. Freely you've received, freely give. Withholding grace speaks more to your character than to the recipient's worth, so be known as one who is gracious and generous in spirit.

If it is within your power to be a blessing, resist the temptation to hold back. Trust My leading, and operate as a conduit through which I can bless others. Closing down that pipeline doesn't actually give you more, but rather it stagnates the flow. So open wide, holding everything loosely. What I prompt you to give won't feel like a loss because of the magnitude of the blessings on their way down the pipeline for you – and for you to share generously.

> *Matthew 10:8 (NIV)* ...*Freely you have received; freely give.*

❋ ❋ ❋

Refining and Protecting

> *Hebrews 12:29 (NET Bible) For our God is indeed a devouring fire.*

Beloved, I AM indeed a consuming fire. The fire of My presence is refining you as flames separate gold from dross. I AM ever purifying and testing you that you might be made more radiant and beautiful – reflecting My glory more and more clearly. Submit to the process, worship Me in the midst, and trust yourself in My hands, knowing I always operate for the good of those who love Me and are called according to My purpose.

As you surrender to My blaze, it also acts as a protection for you, for the enemy has no desire to draw near My scorching flames. In yielding and trusting, you further surrender your protection and well-being to Me, and I will not let you down.

✫ ✫ ✫

I AM Worth Your Extravagant Offering

> *Romans 12:1 (VOICE) Brothers and sisters, in light of all I have shared with you about God's mercies, I urge you to offer your bodies as a living and holy sacrifice to God, a sacred offering that brings Him pleasure; this is your reasonable, essential worship.*

Beloved, you are a living sacrifice, beautiful and pleasing to Me. You are poured out before Me, and the sweet aroma of your worship is like incense before My throne. You dance among the flames of My presence, arms lifted high in reverent praise. I cannot look away, for you have captivated My gaze. Behold you are beautiful My love – altogether lovely!

Your sacrifice, a surrendered heart, is extravagant and so worthy. In fact, I accept nothing less. You give your best to Me just as I give and have given My best to you. We are ensconced in our love – passionate and true. Ever burning like a jealous flame, My heart is steadfast to you. So pour it out beloved. Your heart – your worship – isn't wasted. I AM worth your extravagant offering. I AM consuming you.

> *Leviticus 9:24 (GW) Fire came out from the Lord's presence and consumed the burnt offering and the pieces of fat on the altar. When all the people saw this, they shouted and bowed with their faces touching the ground.*

❃ ❃ ❃

Beautiful Sacrifice

> *Song of Solomon 8:6 (VOICE) Set me as a seal over your heart; wear me as an emblem on your arm For love is as strong as death, and jealousy is as relentless as the grave. Love flares up like a blazing fire, a very ardent flame.*

Beloved, the depths of My love for you are truly unfathomable. My passion burns brightly for you, so brightly its glory fills the earth. May My passion ignite and stir your own, beloved. Match your passion to Mine, allowing yourself to hold nothing back.

May your ardent affection cause you to pour out yourself completely as a living sacrifice before Me. I will receive you, beloved. The flames of My love are consuming your beautiful sacrifice – so sweet and pleasant before Me.

❃ ❃ ❃

Beautiful Life

> *Psalm 16:11 (VOICE) …You direct me on the path that leads to a beautiful life. As I walk with You, the pleasures are never-ending, and I know true joy and contentment.*

Beloved, My plans for you are beautiful and will fill you with more contentment than you can begin to imagine. Release yourself completely to My care and My loving hands. My plans for you are good plans – plans to prosper you and not to harm you, plans for hope and a future.

Allow Me to direct your path. Even in the trials, joy will steady you as you willingly yield to Me. Beautiful is the life I have for you. Rejoice in it and in how I move in and through you, beloved.

> *Jeremiah 29:11 (NIV) For I know the plans I have for you," declares the Lord, "plans to prosper you and not to harm you, plans to give you hope and a future.*
>
> *Isaiah 30:21 (VOICE) Your ears will hear sweet words behind you: "Go this way. There is your path; this is how you should go" whenever you must decide whether to turn to the right or the left.*

※ ※ ※

Priestly Role, a Surrendered Life

> *Numbers 4:16 (GW) "Eleazar, son of the priest Aaron, will be in charge of the oil for the lamps, the sweet-smelling incense, the daily grain offering, and the anointing oil. He is in charge of the whole tent and everything in it, the holy place and its contents."*

Beloved, you are called to be a priest – one who surrenders their life in service to Me. And part of a priest's role is to facilitate My presence – the oil of My anointing – that My glory might burn brightly. Another part is to lead worship by example, not just in praise, but in life of worship – a heart fixed on Me as a sacrifice, a holy offering, continually and willingly surrendering control to Me.

As you release the reins of your life to Me, you demonstrate to others that I AM trustworthy. No word need be spoken. I assure you, people see. Not only do they see, but they watch to see how I will respond. It is then that they see My love and the inner strength, peace, and joy I bring. So live well, beloved, and walk in the priestly role you've been called to.

> *1 Peter 2:9 (ESV) But you are a chosen race, a royal priesthood, a holy nation, a people for his own possession, that you may proclaim the excellencies of him who called you out of darkness into his marvelous light.*

❈ ❈ ❈

All I AM Chooses You

> *Revelation 22:13 (TLV) I am the Alpha and the Omega, the First and the Last, the Beginning and the End.*

Beloved, I AM full of apparent contradictions: I AM the first and the last, a pillar of fire as well as a cloud, and my voice is a whisper and booming thunder. It is because I cannot be contained or defined. I AM bigger than you know or could comprehend. I defy definition.

But you do not need to have plumbed the depths of all I AM to know I AM for you. I AM faithful to the last. I AM holy and righteous, fair and just, and I love you with an everlasting love. I AM steadfast and unchanging. I AM on your side. All I AM is a God who loves you profoundly and longs to be in relationship with you and to see you prosper.

My cry throughout time (and recorded in scripture) is simply that I would be your God and you would be My people. My heart has not changed – will not change. Love Me and choose Me, day after day, moment after moment, beloved, just as I choose you.

※ ※ ※

Far More With You

> *Exodus 14:19 (VOICE) God's messenger, who had been out front leading the people of Israel, moved to*

> *protect the rear of the company; the cloud pillar moved with him from the front to the back of them.*

Beloved, I AM your covering. My heavenly hosts stand at the ready, guarding and protecting – alert and ready to execute My command. Our desire is to protect you from that which would seek your harm. I AM on your side and the hosts of heaven act on My behalf.

Even though you cannot physically see My presence before you, I AM always with you. My hosts ever surround you. Truly, beloved, there are far more with you than against you. Ask Me to open your eyes that you might see.

> *2 Kings 6:16-17 (VOICE) Elisha: Have no fear. We have more on our side than they do. {praying} O Eternal One, I ask You to allow my servant to see heavenly realities. The Eternal awakened Elisha's servant so that he could see. This is what he saw: the mountain was covered with horses and chariots of fire surrounding Elisha.*

※ ※ ※

Taste and See

> *Psalm 34:8 (NOG) Taste and see that Yahweh is good. Blessed is the person who takes refuge in him.*

Beloved, taste and see that I AM good. Evidence of My goodness surrounds you. Try Me. Put your faith in Me, and release the outcome. See how I move. I AM good and I love you. Blessed are those who rest in Me.

I AM your rock and your firm foundation. I AM unshakable and immovable. Find shelter under My wings. Let Me be your hiding place. Let Me be the one you run to. Taste and see, beloved. I AM faithful to the end.

※ ※ ※

Explore with Me

> *Isaiah 45:3 (VOICE) I will give you hidden treasures and wealth tucked away in secret places; I will reveal them to you. Then you will know that I am the Eternal, the God of Israel, who calls you by name.*

Beloved, I have so much more for you – things below the surface, outside your immediate natural understanding. Will you go deep with Me? Will you allow Me to give you revelation? Will you choose to take the time – make the time – for us to be together?

Seek Me as you would immeasurable riches, for I AM more worthy and considerably more satisfying than such. Explore with Me. Together let us plumb the depths of My mysteries that I may share with you and teach you as I have promised.

> *Proverbs 3:13-15 (ESV) Blessed is the one who finds wisdom, and the one who gets understanding,*

> *for the gain from her is better than gain from silver and her profit better than gold. She is more precious than jewels, and nothing you desire can compare with her.*

❈ ❈ ❈

I AM the Richest of Fare

> *Psalm 37:3 (TPT) Keep trusting in the Lord and do what is right in His eyes. Fix your heart on the promises of God and you will be secure, Feasting on His faithfulness.*

Beloved, feast on Me and on My goodness for I AM the richest of fare. Delight yourself in Me. Know My heart that you might act rightly and do that which is pleasing to Me. Trust Me and lean on Me, knowing I will not let you down for I AM faithful.

My promises are yes and amen. See them as done, beloved, for the moment they leave My mouth, they are as good as such. Let the surety of them anchor you and provide stability as the enemy seeks to agitate and distract you. I AM faithful. I AM true. I watch over My word to perform it. Trust in Me.

❈ ❈ ❈

Let Victory Be Your Song

> *2 Timothy 1:7 (VOICE) You see, God did not give us a cowardly spirit but a powerful, loving, and disciplined spirit.*

Beloved, let My love for you embolden you. Let it fill you with confidence in Me. You walk in victory when you walk with Me. Refuse discouragement. The enemy will always try to distract you with seeming failures, and he loves to malign My character. But you know and walk in Truth.

Let victory be your song. Let My joy wrap through your soul, filling you with strength. Radiate the assurance of one who knows Me. Be filled with the knowledge of Me, and be overwhelmed by My love.

* * *

Peace and Joy Will Reign

> *Malachi 3:12 (AMP) "All nations shall call you happy and blessed, for you shall be a land of delight," says the Lord of hosts.*

Beloved, choose Me – dedicate yourself and your resources to Me – and see how I will move. Your land will flourish, your people will prosper, and peace and joy will reign.

Those who love Me, declare it as so. Command the atmosphere. Come into agreement with My vision for your land. Declare over your nation that it shall be a people that serve the Lord. Minister to their hearts, that they might see and know Me.

* * *

Strengthened by Trials

> *James 1:3-4 (TPT) For you know that when your faith is tested it stirs up power within you to endure all things. And then as your endurance grows even stronger it will release perfection into every part of your being until there is nothing missing and nothing lacking.*

Beloved, the trials you have walked through have served their purpose. They have stretched your faith and enlarged your ability to believe in Me for both the miraculous and the mundane. You have tasted and seen. You know that I AM faithful. Your confidence in My character is steadfast, for I AM unimpugnable.

You've learned by experience that worrying and wondering are wastes of time and energy, and in wisdom you simply look to Me and follow My lead. As a result, I AM pouring out increase over you, for you are faithful to Me, and I cherish that. I do not take lightly the cost that was required from you to get to this point. Though I know it was needful, it didn't make it easy to watch as you struggled. But you were tried by fire and have been strengthened for it. You are My joy.

✵ ✵ ✵

Unflinching Faith

> *Daniel 3:17 (TLV) If it is so, our God whom we serve is able to save us from the furnace of blazing fire and He will deliver us out of your hand, O king.*

Beloved, refuse to allow circumstances to alter your faith. Be steadfast – strong and determined – and have unflinching faith. Stand fast like Shadrach, Meshach, and Abed-nego in the face of seemingly impossible obstacles, and declare that I AM faithful regardless of circumstance.

I AM with you, I never leave you, I love you and desire good for you. Rest in Me, knowing that whether or not I choose the outcome you desire, I always choose you and My heart towards you is good. I see things you don't see and cause all things to work together for good.

> *Romans 8:28 (VOICE) We are confident that God is able to orchestrate everything to work toward something good and beautiful when we love Him and accept His invitation to live according to His plan.*

※ ※ ※

Move Others as You Have Moved Me

> *Matthew 20:34 (VOICE) Jesus had compassion on them and touched their eyes. Immediately they could see, and so they followed Him.*

Beloved, I love you. Therefore My heart is easily moved with compassion toward you. You don't need to beg or plead or bargain. I cannot be controlled or manipulated, but I love you, and I love you deeply. You move Me deeply.

So expect My touch of compassion in your life and on your heart, beloved, and then respond. When I touch you, you are changed, and that change moves you just as you moved Me. When you are rightly aligned, you reflect Me and My heart of compassion, and so in turn you will touch others. Freely you have received, freely give.

It is worth the cost to extend your hand and bless another. Do not withhold. Reflect Me and My heart to give freely and generously to the kind and the cruel. Be My light shining forth, and move others as you have moved Me.

> *Matthew 5:44-48 (GW) But I tell you this: Love your enemies, and pray for those who persecute you. In this way you show that you are children of your Father in heaven. He makes his sun rise on people whether they are good or evil. He lets rain fall on them whether they are just or unjust. If you love those who love you, do you deserve a reward? Even the tax collectors do that! Are you doing anything remarkable if you welcome only your friends? Everyone does that! That is why you must be perfect as your Father in heaven is perfect.*

❊ ❊ ❊

Bathe Luxuriously in My Word

> *Psalm 119:130 (VOICE) When Your words are unveiled, light shines forth; they bring understanding to the simple.*

Beloved, I bring wisdom through the revelation of My Word. My word is a conduit for truth and understanding. As you wash yourself in it, taking the time to luxuriously bathe, I impart to you via divine revelation truths you have not yet known.

Seek Me, beloved. My word is My heart laid bare. Know Me. Hear My heart cry and feel the depth of My longing for the hearts of My people. For the more of Me that is hidden in their hearts, the more radiant they become, and that glow draws others home to Me. A beautiful gift from My beloved to Me.

※ ※ ※

Look to Me

> *Isaiah 33:22 (NLT) For the Lord is our judge, our lawgiver, and our king. He will care for us and save us.*

Beloved, resist the urge to lean on yourself or to look to a human to care and provide. For ultimately I AM the only one who is truly reliable and steadfast, and though I may work through those around you to minister to your needs, always remember I AM the source.

I AM Palet (your deliverer) and El Elyon (God Most High). I AM where your help comes from. I AM Elohim Mishpat (God of Judgment/Justice). I AM Elohim Emeth (True God/God of Truth). I make wrong things right. I save the lives of My children, and I cherish and protect them. I AM their provider (YHVH Yireh) and I AM YHVH Nissi (the Lord your banner/your victory/miracle). Depend on Me.

> *Psalm 121:1-2 (TLB) Shall I look to the mountain gods for help? No! My help is from Jehovah who made the mountains! And the heavens too!*

❈ ❈ ❈

Come Soar in My Love

> *Exodus 13:22 (GW) The column of smoke was always in front of the people during the day. The column of fire was always there at night.*

Beloved, I AM always with you, and I will never leave you. Abide with Me. Absorb the peace found in My presence, and let your spirit take flight. As you soar with Me, feel the wind of My Spirit. Let Me bring you higher and higher. Trust Me.

Place your hand in Mine, beloved. Let Me carry you away. Behold, you are beautiful, My love, and you have captured My heart. You have captivated My gaze. You are the apple of My eye, the center of my world. Just as young lovers cannot get enough of each other's presence, so I long to be with you. Will you abide with Me? Come soar in My love.

❈ ❈ ❈

Cultivate a Place for Me to Dwell

> *Exodus 20:20 (VOICE) Moses: Don't be afraid. These powerful manifestations are God's way of instilling awe and fear in you so that you will not sin; He is testing you for your own good.*

Beloved, be mindful not to allow familiarity to breed contempt. I AM still God. I love you and cherish intimacy with you. I've provided grace for you and granted you forgiveness, but at no point have I relaxed My standards on what is good and what is evil.

The enemy will tempt you to flirt with the line between sin and what is permissible, but if your heart truly knows who I AM and you love Me, you will not want to grieve Me by following the letter of the law rather than the spirit. Know My heart and strive to be like Me. Cultivate a place for Me to dwell within you.

※ ※ ※

Be at Peace

> *Matthew 6:27 (CSB) Can any of you add one moment to his life-span by worrying?*

Beloved, refuse to allow the enemy to tempt you into useless cycles of fruitless energy by worrying. Trust in Me. I AM sovereign. I AM almighty. Nothing shocks or surprises Me. Nothing catches Me off guard. Rest in that knowledge.

You don't have to be in control or even try to understand all the whys of a situation. You can simply rest, knowing that One who is for you does know, so trust Me to lead, guide, and protect you in the midst of it. Lean on Me. Rest in Me. Be at peace.

❊ ❊ ❊

With Me Nothing is Out of Reach

> *Philippians 4:13 (AMP) I can do all things [which He has called me to do] through Him who strengthens and empowers me [to fulfill His purpose —I am self-sufficient in Christ's sufficiency; I am ready for anything and equal to anything through Him who infuses me with inner strength and confident peace.]*

Beloved, I AM greater than you know and your strength is found in Me. I AM filled with seeming contradictions, using the foolish things to confound the wise. So rest in Me and grow strong. In your weakness, My strength is made perfect. You don't have to be big and strong for I AM, and you have simply to be like Me.

Walk in My ways, follow My heart, and trust in Me. Then see what I do. Suddenly the impossible is possible. Don't discount any possibility because with Me nothing is out of reach. Yield to My will and My plans, and you will see Me move through you in ways you couldn't even imagine. Breathe Me in beloved. Worship with all your heart. Walk confidently in Me.

❊ ❊ ❊

Walk in Purity of Heart, Mind, and Spirit

> *1 Peter 1:15 (VOICE) Since the One who called you is holy, be holy in all you do.*

Beloved, it's time to step up to a new level. Things that were permissible in the old season must be released for you to move forward into all I've called you to. It's time to let go or be dragged behind and miss My perfect will. Be holy, beloved, for I AM holy. Check your heart, your mind, and your deeds to make certain they are rightly aligned with Me. You know My voice.

Choose that which is best, not that which is acceptable. My love for you is unconditional, but the fulfillment you will experience from walking in the calling I have for you far surpasses the temporary "pleasures" of that which seeks to waylay you. Be holy, beloved. Allow the refining of My Spirit to do its work. Walk in purity of heart, mind, and spirit.

✵ ✵ ✵

Be Excited and Stay the Course

> *1 Corinthians 2:9 (AMP) but just as it is written [in Scripture], "Things which the eye has not seen and the ear has not heard, And which have not entered the heart of man, All that God has prepared for those who love Him [who hold Him in affectionate reverence, who obey Him, and who gratefully recognize the benefits that He has bestowed]."*

Beloved, you cannot begin to imagine what I have planned for you. Fear not, for I have prepared you and am readying you, and you will operate in My strength. But what is coming is glorious! Stay the course. Refuse to be waylaid. I have promised you good things – a hope and a future – and I AM true to My word.

Let your excitement and anticipation build. I AM glorious, and when I move, I change things. I AM taking you from glory to glory. Prepare to be astonished at all I will do through you. You have yielded, and you have chosen to be purified. See what I will do! Be excited and stay the course. The best is yet to come.

※ ※ ※

Giving and Receiving Honor

> *1 Samuel 2:30 (AMP) ...But now the Lord declares, 'Far be it from Me—for those who honor Me I will honor, and those who despise Me will be insignificant and contemptible.*

Beloved, when you give honor where honor is due, you are also honoring Me. It is a sign you recognize those I have raised up and are coming into agreement with Me. It is more powerful than you know and requires humility to walk out.

And beloved, when you are the one rightly receiving honor, remember then, too, that you honor Me in receiving it. You are coming into agreement with what (and who) I have deemed worthy of exalting. Do so with humility, but receive the honor given, knowing it not only blesses Me to see you honored and acknowledged, but it also gives Me glory.

❊ ❊ ❊

Who I Give Honor to is Honored

Proverbs 16:31 (GW) Silver hair is a beautiful crown found in a righteous life.

Beloved, embrace the sign of wisdom and experience. It is a crown of honor. Even in moments when others refuse to give honor or bring dishonor (either ignorantly or intentionally), it does not change the fact that I honor the wisdom that comes through years spent with Me. If others choose not to align, that is an indicator of their own state, not yours. For one to whom I give honor is honored.

{praying} Sensing a prayer over the elders that they would have grace and patience with the younger generation – as they rush about often barely pausing to breathe and who too often in arrogance refuse wise counsel – continue to gently persist in giving it, speaking words of truth and life. As you echo the Voice of heaven and His heart, your words and actions have impact whether you get to see that impact or not. Trust it is there, and continue in obedience reflecting His heart. For it is vital to the body of Christ. Your role is vital. You are a blessing. Thank you.

❊ ❊ ❊

Tender of Your Heart

> *Proverbs 3:5 (TPT) Trust in the Lord completely, and do not rely on your own opinions. With all your heart rely on him to guide you, and he will lead you in every decision you make.*

Beloved, you are safe in My hands. Trust Me with your heart, your life, your plans. Look at the intricacies of My creation – the beauty of how the flowers and trees burst with the fragrances I've given them, the richness of the colors, even the textures of the creatures I've created.

I AM all about detail. I don't overlook anything, and nothing is beneath My notice. Every part of you is safe with Me. I will saturate you with My love. Trust yourself in My hands. Let Me be the tender of your heart.

❈ ❈ ❈

Train Your Gaze on Me

> *Exodus 23:13 (VOICE) Be careful to do all that I have instructed you. Do not even acknowledge the names of other gods or let their names spill from your lips.*

Beloved, refuse to acknowledge the enemy by giving him credit in your life. I AM your God, and I will not share with another. Resist the urge to point at his opposition and use it as a barometer for your walk, saying, "I know I am doing something right because he is opposing me." The enemy will always oppose you because I love you. He will always lay traps to ensnare you because you are precious to me.

Look to Me, beloved, and keep your eyes fixed. Trust that I will guide you with My eye. Train your gaze upon Me, never allowing it to waver. I AM the Lord your God. I AM the faithful God, keeping My promises from generation to generation. My promise you have. My love you have. My acceptance you have. I AM all you need.

> *Psalm 32:8 (NKJV) I will instruct you and teach you in the way you should go; I will guide you with My eye.*
>
> *Deuteronomy 7:9 (NLT) Understand, therefore, that the Lord your God is indeed God. He is the faithful God who keeps his covenant for a thousand generations and lavishes his unfailing love on those who love him and obey his commands.*

✸ ✸ ✸

Let My Love Nourish You

> *Galatians 5:22 (AMP) But the fruit of the Spirit [the result of His presence within us] is... goodness...*

Beloved, let fruit pour forth from a rich relationship with Me. I AM always here, I AM always ready, and I always love you. Reach out to Me. Let Me be your nourishment. As the saying goes, "You are what you eat," so dine on My Word as the choicest of meats, and drink deeply of My saturating love.

Then let goodness pour forth from your life – the fingerprints of Me made manifest. Bear fruit, beloved. Operate in integrity simply because I see, and you desire to walk in a manner pleasing to Me. Do it with joy knowing the pleasure you bring. Let your light shine brightly. Set an example to others. Walk in the fullness of all I've made you for.

❈ ❈ ❈

Worth Knowing

> *Isaiah 58:11 (NLT) The Lord will guide you continually, giving you water when you are dry and restoring your strength. You will be like a well-watered garden, like an ever-flowing spring.*

Beloved, I AM all that you need. Rest in Me and let Me provide and heal, refresh and restore, build up and inspire, teach and reveal. I long to dwell with you, to have you abide in My presence, that we might commune together and nourish each other's hearts.

You cannot imagine how much you please Me – how your fumbling attempts bless Me. Stop being so hard on yourself and trust My love for you. Trust that I AM good and that I AM looking for the good in you. I AM not looking for reasons to be angry, beloved. Nor am I eagerly awaiting standing in judgment of you. Refuse to allow the world's view of who I AM to color your view. Know Me and know My heart. Like you, I AM worth knowing.

❊ ❊ ❊

Safe in My Hands

> *Isaiah 26:3 (VOICE) You will keep the peace, a perfect peace, for all who trust in You, for those who dedicate their hearts and minds to You.*

Beloved, take your hands off the wheel and let Me drive. You don't need to be in control to be safe. On the contrary, trying to be only brings the illusion of control. Like Dumbo's feather, the illusion of control brings you a sense of peace, but it is not founded in truth. You are a child of the Light. Truth is your inheritance.

Beloved, release it all to Me. In My hands is the only place you are truly safe. As you shift control into My capable hands, it may feel awkward and uncomfortable at first, but know that, over time, the removal of the burden it has lifted from you will feel more freeing than you can imagine.

Remember, beloved, that I AM the first and the last – the beginning and the end. I see it all. I know what is coming and know exactly where you should be positioned and what provision you'll need. As you trust Me and yield to Me, I make you ready. I AM worthy of your trust. Lay down the idol of needing to understand, and fully release yourself into My care. For I love you, and I will never leave you. You are safe in My hands.

❊ ❊ ❊

An Irrefutable Testimony

> *Matthew 19:21 (AMP) Jesus answered him, "If you wish to be perfect [that is, have the spiritual maturity that accompanies godly character with no moral or ethical deficiencies], go and sell what you have and give [the money] to the poor, and you will have treasure in heaven; and come, follow Me [becoming My disciple, believing and trusting in Me and walking the same path of life that I walk]."*

Beloved, hold nothing back from Me. Follow hard after Me. Allow Me to work My perfect purpose in and through you. As you allow Me unrestrained access, My burning passion and the fire of My Holy Spirit refines and matures you, bringing forth your inherent strength and beauty of character.

Then as you walk in My favor – as one with unreserved access to the King – I will cause the miraculous to follow you. For your faith has declared My faithfulness; thus My power will make manifest the fruit of your faith, making your life and your walk an irrefutable testimony of who I AM.

❋ ❋ ❋

Enforcing Your Claim

> *Joshua 1:3 (AMP) I have given you every place on which the sole of your foot treads, just as I promised to Moses.*

Beloved, you are claiming territory for Me. As you exude My light, every place your foot shall step forces darkness to flee. My angelic hosts enforce your claim as you walk, reclaiming step-by-step – forcing back the darkness that seeks to encroach.

You walk in might, for My presence surrounds you. So be intentional and unafraid, letting your light shine that My glory may be made manifest in the earth.

※ ※ ※

Be Fruitful and Multiply

> *Isaiah 53:2 (NLT) My servant grew up in the Lord's presence like a tender green shoot, like a root in dry ground. There was nothing beautiful or majestic about his appearance, nothing to attract us to him.*

Beloved, like My Son, grow in My presence. Like a tender shoot, I will protect you from the elements and nurture you to your full potential. For I see you even now as a grown tree – full and lush, bearing much fruit. The capacity for life within you is great. Be mindful to cultivate that growth – to nourish it with My word, water it with My Spirit, and fortify it with My presence.

For the life within you is greater than just yourself. Allow it to multiply and bring forth increase. Be fruitful and multiply. Refuse to allow yourself to become dry and withered. Find the time – indeed make the time – do whatever it takes to carry what

I AM bringing forth through you to full term. Behold I AM doing a new thing. Will you not know it? *[Sensing Him smiling as He asks because He already knows you will say yes – a thousand times yes.]*

※ ※ ※

Boldly Evident

> *Ephesians 6:13, 17 (AMP) Therefore, put on the complete armor of God, so that you will be able to [successfully] resist and stand your ground in the evil day [of danger]...And take the helmet of salvation...*

Beloved, you have the mind of Christ. Refuse to allow the enemy to set up camp in your thought life. He may pester and poke, but only you can grant him access. So send him packing. Take the thought bombs he lobs at you captive. Refuse to take the bait.

Worry is not from Me. Fear is not from Me. Lust is not from Me. Greed is not from Me. Beloved, you know Me. Filter your thoughts through My Word and My heart, and you will clearly know which ideas originate from above and which come from below. Think on that which is good and perfect and true, assume positive intent, and walk in integrity of character that the joy of your salvation might be boldly evident for all to see.

※ ※ ※

Confident Authority and Uprightness

> *Psalm 84:11 (VOICE) For the Eternal God is a sun and a shield. The Eternal grants favor and glory; He doesn't deny any good thing to those who live with integrity.*

Beloved, stand fast in My truth – armed and ready to withstand and not be shaken in the face of the evil one. I stand with you and enforce your victory. No weapon formed against you will prosper, for you are Mine beloved and My covering rests upon you.

So walk in confident authority and uprightness, reflecting My character and nature that I might be made known. Extend grace even as you stand firm with your sword of truth and shield of faith to hand. Victory is Mine and it is assured.

❉ ❉ ❉

Carrier of My Living Water

> *Revelation 22:1 (VOICE) My heavenly guide brought me to the river of pure living waters, shimmering as brilliantly as crystal. It flowed out from the throne of God and of the Lamb,*

Beloved, My living water flows fresh and clear from heaven, raining down on you. Raise your arms and open your heart and receive My flow. Drink deeply, beloved, and allow the refreshing, life-giving flow to saturate every area of your being and your life. You are a beautiful vessel, beloved. Let Me fill you to overflowing.

And then, beloved, pour it forth on the dry and cracked hearts and places and situations around you. You are a conduit – a carrier of Me – to a lost and dying world that desperately needs a touch from Me. Be that touch. Minister My love, My healing, My refreshing, My living water, and bring forth life – and life abundantly – all around you.

※ ※ ※

Make Knowing My Heart a Priority

> *Song of Solomon 4:12 (VOICE) You are a locked garden, my sister, my bride, open only to me; a spring closed up tight, a sealed fountain.*

Beloved, I will not share first place in your heart with another. You are My beautiful treasure, apple of My eye, the center of My world. Truly, you cannot fathom the depths of My love for you nor the lengths to which I will go for you. You are not something I take lightly.

So, beloved, be mindful not to take Me lightly nor the things that are important to Me. In the same way that it hurts you if someone important to you dismisses something deeply meaningful to you, it crushes Me as well. You are made in My image. The hurts you feel are ones I feel too, as are the longings. Make knowing My heart a priority. The joy that will come from the intimacies we share the deeper we go are greater than you can imagine.

✿ ✿ ✿

Relentlessly Seek Me and Ask for Wisdom

> *1 Kings 3:10 (TLB) The Lord was pleased with his reply and was glad that Solomon had asked for wisdom.*

Beloved, ask Me. Ask Me for wisdom. In the asking you show that you are laying down self-sufficiency and acknowledging your need of Me. This is good both in that it is to your benefit to seek Me, and also in that it is beautiful to My heart when you seek Me and My thoughts and insights.

Yes, My ways are higher and often difficult to understand, but as our intimacy grows, I am able to share more and more with you. The question is not whether there is more for Me to share with you, but rather how much time you want to spend with Me, for what I have to share is limitless. I love to reveal My mysteries with My trusted and faithful ones who relentlessly seek Me. It is your choice whether or not you want that to be you. *[Feeling Him gently smile as He says that.]*

✿ ✿ ✿

Be Radiant without Shame

> *Psalm 34:5 (GW) All who look to him will be radiant. Their faces will never be covered with shame.*

Beloved, shame is not from Me. The price has already been paid for you to be free. *[Seeing what appears to be a cloak being removed and understanding it's a covering of shame being removed]*.

Look to Me, beloved. Allow the glory of My presence to reflect on your face. Be radiant without shame or fear darkening your countenance. Refuse to allow the lies of the enemy to cloud who you are and change your reflection. You are beautiful, beloved, fearfully and wonderfully made. Allow My glory to shine on and in you.

※ ※ ※

Allow My Perfect Love to Impart Perfect Peace

> *John 14:27 (TLB) I am leaving you with a gift — peace of mind and heart! And the peace I give isn't fragile like the peace the world gives. So don't be troubled or afraid.*

Beloved, peace is My gift to you. As you rest in the knowledge that I AM sovereign, I AM for you, I AM covering you, and I AM working all things for good; you can relax into that place of abandoned control, leaving the details to Me and receiving for yourself the peace that surpasses all understanding. For I AM faithful, and the peace I bring is one that combats chaos – a strong and active peace, unshakable and abiding.

When you truly comprehend and accept who I AM, you can stop trying to manage and manipulate the details and release them to Me, knowing My ability to handle them far exceeds your own both because of My view (I see the beginning and the end) and because of My wisdom (I see the inner workings and know the secret thoughts of men's hearts). And when all that is framed in My deep and unending love for you, you no longer will feel the need to usurp My role, but instead will happily place it in My hands and skip off with the lightness and joy of the child you are called to be. Beloved, allow My perfect love to impart perfect peace.

* * *

Covenant Strength Shining Through You

> *2 Corinthians 12:9 (AMP) but He has said to me, "My grace is sufficient for you [My lovingkindness and My mercy are more than enough—always available—regardless of the situation]; for [My] power is being perfected [and is completed and shows itself most effectively] in [your] weakness." Therefore, I will all the more gladly boast in my weaknesses, so that the power of Christ [may completely enfold me and] may dwell in me.*

Beloved, don't be tempted to see your weaknesses as flaws or shortcomings, but rather as areas for My strength to shine through you. My grace is sufficient. Refuse to be tempted into pride by wanting to be seen as "capable," but rather seek to be known for being completely reliant on Me. That is a legacy worth having.

Boast in Me and in My power, for I AM more than enough and delight in showing who I AM. You need not fight or argue or scramble for Me to be faithful, for My covenant with you extends generation to generation of those who love Me. Let Me be magnified in you.

❊ ❊ ❊

My Promises are Assured

> *Psalm 103:4 (AMPC) Who redeems your life from the pit and corruption, Who beautifies, dignifies, and crowns you with loving-kindness and tender mercy;*

Beloved, I love you too much to leave you on a path of hurt and destruction. I made a way and have drawn you to Myself. I have crowned you with unfailing love and compassion. You are priceless to Me and worth dying for.

Just as My covenant with Abraham is unconditional, so is My covenant of love with those who've chosen Me. Simply cling to Me and trust that My promises - Blood-covered and enforced - will not return void. I watch over to perform them and delight in bringing them to pass, for it pleases Me to bless My children. Rest in My promises, beloved, for they are assured.

> *Genesis 15:17 (GW) The sun had gone down, and it was dark. Suddenly a smoking oven and a flaming torch passed between the animal pieces.*

❊ ❊ ❊

Shine and Shine Brightly

> *Exodus 3:14 (TLB)* "'*The Sovereign God,*'" *was the reply. "Just say, 'I Am has sent me!'*

Beloved, you move under My authority and by My command. Never forget the level of authority you are operating under. There is no greater power in heaven or on earth for I AM sovereign. I AM that I AM.

I AM the Eternal One who sees all, knows all, and loves you boundlessly. Despite the vast knowledge at My hand and all the things, people, and situations vying for My attention, you, beloved, have captured My gaze. In the midst of it all I pause to tend to My beloved. To encourage you in all I have called you to.

See by My actions how precious you are to Me. Hear with your heart My instructions and execute them without hesitation or concern, knowing I AM with you. Don't hold back, beloved. Shine, and shine brightly. Be all I have called you to, and let yourself soar in My presence and on My wings.

* * *

Ask

> *2 Kings 6:17 (GW)* Then Elisha prayed, "Lord, please open his eyes so that he may see." The Lord opened the servant's eyes and let him see. The

> *mountain around Elisha was full of fiery horses and chariots.*

Beloved, ask Me to see. I have given you eyes to see and ears to hear so you are able. There is nothing to fear, for I AM with you always. Truly, legions of angels stand at the ready, engaging on your behalf at My request in response to your prayers. So ask, beloved.

Ask to see. Ask for help. Seek Me - My hand and My assistance. I AM YHVH Sabaoth, the Lord of Hosts - leader of the heavenly armies. Nothing can stand against me and succeed. So stand with Me.

Mirror My countenance - one of peace and love firmly rooted in truth. Be like Me. Love as if you'll never get hurt. Eyes wide open. Knowing your heart is in My hands and is safe there. Your pain is never wasted, beloved. I collect every tear, so priceless is your heart to me. Trust Me and trust My plans for you, for I AM God and I AM good.

❖ ❖ ❖

See Me As I AM

> *Psalm 96:6-7 (VOICE) Honor and majesty precede Him; strength and beauty infuse His holy sanctuary.*

Beloved, see Me as I AM – high and lifted up. Honor and majesty go before Me, My grandeur and glory fill the heavens and the earth. I AM vast and unchangeable. You can spend the rest of your life attempting to plumb the depths of Me and still only scratch the surface.

Behold, beloved, the beauty of my majesty. Be strengthened in My presence and encouraged by a deeper understanding of who I AM. As you understand in greater measure how enormous and truly powerful I AM, you can't help but worship - can't help but trust. When you have glimpsed My heart, you cannot help but understand that I AM God and I AM good.

❊ ❊ ❊

I Still Choose You

> *Revelation 2:4 (TPT) But I have this against you: you have abandoned the passionate love you had for me at the beginning.*

Beloved, I will not settle for anything less than your whole heart. I'm not an old shoe to grow comfortable in. I AM worth your fiery passion and abandoned restraint. There is no need or reason to hold back from Me. I want all of you and I love you unconditionally. I AM not shocked that you are not perfect. I love you - flaws, imperfections, and all.

I still choose you. Knowing everything about you - every time you'll choose to wound me, every time you'll prefer to pour out your affections to someone or something who does not hold you at the immeasurable value that I do – even knowing all that, I still choose you. I still love you. I AM not angry or upset with you. You hold My heart, and my grace for you exceeds comprehension.

※ ※ ※

Refuse To Be Silent

> *Isaiah 62:6 (AMP) On your walls, O Jerusalem, I have appointed and stationed watchmen (prophets), Who will never keep silent day or night; You who profess the Lord, take no rest for yourselves,*

Beloved, be relentless in your prayers. The enemy will always be persistent and tactical in his attacks, so be persistent and tactical in yours by staying focused and intentional in prayer. Allow My Holy Spirit to lead and guide you. Refuse to be silenced. Cry out. Declare truth and life.

I AM the way. I AM the truth. I AM the life. Declare the truth of Who I AM and the authority I hold in every situation and circumstance. Nothing is too hard for Me. I AM mighty. I AM strong. I AM the Lord of Heavenly Armies, and I will not be defeated.

※ ※ ※

Allow My Spirit to Saturate You

> *Song of Solomon 4:15 (VOICE) My bride, you are a fountain in a garden, a well of life-giving water flowing down from Lebanon.*

Beloved, you are a well of life, deep and true - your capacity great, your water fresh and pure. Allow the life within you to gurgle up and overflow, bringing life to all those around you – tender shoots of green and brilliant colors of wildflower life surrounding you.

Feed on Me in our times alone. Allow Me to nourish and replenish you, beloved, that your well will never run dry. Wait on Me. Soak in My presence. Abide in Me. Allow My Spirit to overtake you and saturate your soul.

※ ※ ※

I AM Good

> *Psalm 143:10 (TLB) Help me to do your will, for you are my God. Lead me in good paths, for your Spirit is good.*

Beloved, one truth you can always rest in is the knowledge that I AM good. My heart is good. My intentions are good. My plans for you are good. The very definition of the word is based on My character: righteous, just, honorable, true, honest, upright, virtuous. I AM all this and more!

Because of all I AM, there is none more trustworthy than Me. You need not wonder if you can release your perceived control to My hands, for there is no doubt that I AM good. I cherish you and have good plans for you. They may not always be easy, but walk them through hand-in-hand with Me, knowing that in the end you will see they are good.

※ ※ ※

Bringing Forth the Good

> *2 Corinthians 12:7 (AMP) Because of the surpassing greatness and extraordinary nature of the revelations [which I received from God], for this reason, to keep me from thinking of myself as important, a thorn in the flesh was given to me, a messenger of Satan, to torment and harass me—to keep me from exalting myself!*

Beloved, do not think for one moment that I will not allow you to walk through trials. Even in the natural, children who are indulged and overprotected become spoiled and entitled, so I will allow trials to mold character in your life, and I do this for your own benefit. What I promise you is that I will be with you through them all, I will never give you more than you can handle (with Me), and I will use them all for good.

So as you find yourself in the midst of trials, look for Me there. Seek Me and ask Me what I AM working in the midst of it to grow and bless. Trust that My heart toward you is good and My plans for you are good. Refuse to allow that perspective to waver. The enemy will whisper lies to you about My character, refuse to listen, and cling to Me all the more. I will never leave you or forsake you, so stand fast and allow Me to bring forth the good.

> *James 1:2-5 (VOICE) Don't run from tests and hardships, brothers and sisters. As difficult as they*

are, you will ultimately find joy in them; if you embrace them, your faith will blossom under pressure and teach you true patience as you endure. And true patience brought on by endurance will equip you to complete the long journey and cross the finish line—mature, complete, and wanting nothing. If you don't have all the wisdom needed for this journey, then all you have to do is ask God for it; and God will grant all that you need. He gives lavishly and never scolds you for asking.

❀ ❀ ❀

I AM at Work in You

Philippians 1:6 (VOICE) I am confident that the Creator, who has begun such a great work among you, will not stop in mid-design but will keep perfecting you...

Beloved, trust that I AM at work in you. I never lose Heart or patience with you. I see you for who you truly are and I understand all the intricacies of your heart. You have nothing to fear from Me. I won't tire of you or give up on you, nor am I simply tolerating you. You are My beloved, the apple of My eye and center of My world.

I love you, beloved, and I know what you are capable of because I made you. Trust Me and My leadings as I grow and stretch you into the fullness of all you are called to and all you are able to be. In that place you will find true fulfillment, along with much joy and encouragement along the journey.

❀ ❀ ❀

Refuse to Relinquish Love

> *1 John 2:9 (VOICE) Anyone who says, "I live in the light," but hates his brother or sister is still living in the shadows.*

Beloved, be known by your love. Love is an action. Love costs you something. Love brings light and disperses darkness. Look to Me to see how love is defined: "For this is how God loved the world: He gave His one and only Son, so that everyone who believes in Him will not perish but have eternal life" (John 3:16 NLT).

Refuse to withhold your heart, beloved. Love is always the right choice, but true love is not always gentle. So ask Me for wisdom on how to love, and let Me teach you. And in the moments of sacrifice, heartache and longing, remember I have felt that pain as well, and press into Me, knowing that you are sharing My sufferings and understanding My heart more deeply. But refuse to relinquish love, for it is always the right choice.

※ ※ ※

Choose Compassion, Humility, and Kindness

> *1 Peter 3:8 (AMP) Finally, all of you be like-minded [united in spirit], sympathetic, brotherly, kindhearted [courteous and compassionate toward each other as members of one household], and humble in spirit;*

Beloved, remain humble, intentionally choosing compassion and kindness, and truly operate as brothers and sisters in Christ. You are one Body, called to be known by your love; therefore, lavish it liberally just as I do on My children.

Be intentional about staying in unity. Laying down any need to be right or desire to watch out for your own benefit in lieu of harmony and seeking alignment with Me and My plan. Allow trying moments to build and shape your character, trusting your heart and needs in My capable hands.

❊ ❊ ❊

Let Your Actions Declare My Faithfulness

> *Galatians 5:22 (AMP) But the fruit of the Spirit [the result of His presence within us] is... faithfulness,*

Beloved, I AM forever faithful, setting the example for My children. Allow My Spirit to bring forth faithfulness in you, that you might be focused and singleminded – a picture of loyalty and steadfastness – displaying My character and nature as you reflect Me.

Bear sweet fruit, beloved. You are made in My image, empowered by My Spirit. This character is not beyond your reach. It requires trust in Me – a trust that demonstrates to the world that I AM good and worthy of trust. Your actions will speak far louder than your words ever could, so declare My faithfulness by surrendering your all to Me, knowing I AM full of love and worthy of your heart. Be at peace. I will meet you in that yielded place for I AM good.

> *James 1:8 (VOICE) The splinter of divided loyalty shatters your compass and leaves you dizzy and confused.*

✻ ✻ ✻

Let My Touch on Your Life Testify

> *Psalm 103:5 (AMPC) Who satisfies your mouth [your necessity and desire at your personal age and situation] with good so that your youth, renewed, is like the eagle's [strong, overcoming, soaring]!*

Beloved, allow My Word to satisfy you as the choicest meat and richest honey, and My Spirit to refresh and restore you. Be saturated and rejuvenated in My presence. Allow Me to buoy you, lifting and strengthening you. You are an overcomer!

Let My touch on your life testify to My goodness, announcing to the world that I AM fulfilling, revitalizing, and sustaining. Let My joy radiate from your face that the lightness of your countenance might attest to My love for My children. Let your expectation of good cause you to shine like a beacon of hope in the darkness, for I AM good and I relish delighting Myself in you.

✻ ✻ ✻

I Love a Cheerful Giver

> *1 John 3:17 (TLB) But if someone who is supposed to be a Christian has money enough to live well, and sees a brother in need, and won't help him — how can God's love be within him?*

Beloved, give generously as I give generously to you. Focus with gratitude on the blessings you have rather than allow the enemy to distract you with insatiable desires for what you don't have. I provide for every need. I delight in blessing My children.

So sow as you would reap. Live with an open hand, allowing Me to move through you to bless others just as I bless you through those around you. Refuse to operate from a poverty mindset. Rejoice in your ability to bless others regardless of whether it is something great or small. A heart of obedience is beautiful, and I love a cheerful giver.

> *2 Corinthians 9:7 (AMPC) Let each one [give] as he has made up his own mind and purposed in his heart, not reluctantly or sorrowfully or under compulsion, for God loves (He takes pleasure in, prizes above other things, and is unwilling to abandon or to do without) a cheerful (joyous, "prompt to do it") giver [whose heart is in his giving].*

✣ ✣ ✣

Be My Burning One

> *Hebrews 1:7 (NET) And he says of the angels, "He makes his angels spirits and his ministers a flame of fire,"*

Beloved, My angels still touch coal to lips. Be purified. You are forgiven, refined, and guilt cannot plague you anymore. Choose to be holy as I AM holy. Choose to be tried in the fire. Yield to My process - less of you, more of Me. My refining flames burning away the dross, leaving you purified, sparkling, and new. Burn with passion for Me.

There is no need to resist the flames. Yield to Me and let Me bring forth beauty from the ashes that My glory might shine through. A broken, contrite spirit that seeks hard after Me is the most fragrant offering you can bring. That I will accept. That I will adore. You I cherish, beloved. Be My burning one, with a soul surrendered and a heart ignited for Me.

> *Isaiah 6:6-7 (VOICE) Then one of the flaming creatures flew to me holding a red-hot ember which it had taken from God's table, the temple altar, with a pair of tongs. The creature held it to my lips. Flaming Creature: Look! With the touch of this burning ember on your lips, your guilt is turned away; All your faults and wrongdoings are forgiven.*

> *Psalm 51:16-17 (TLB) You don't want penance; if you did, how gladly I would do it! You aren't*

interested in offerings burned before you on the altar. It is a broken spirit you want—remorse and penitence. A broken and a contrite heart, O God, you will not ignore.

❊ ❊ ❊

Choose the Better Way

Genesis 15:17-18 (AMP) When the sun had gone down and a [deep] darkness had come, there appeared a smoking brazier and a flaming torch which passed between the [divided] pieces [of the animals]. On the same day the Lord made a covenant (promise, pledge) with Abram...

Beloved, My covenant fire stands true today. My promises to you are intact. My love for you is still burning strong - its flame unquenchable. I never forget My word. I watch over it to perform it, patiently waiting to see it come to pass. I hold Myself accountable. You need not wonder if you wait in vain, for as surely as the sun will rise (and indeed even more surely), so My word is steadfast and true.

I breathe on you My breath of life. My words carried on that breath also promise life and life more abundant. Will you rest in My promises? Will you trust in Me? Allow My holy fire to consume and refine you? Yield, beloved. Choose the better way. Surrender to My heart.

❊ ❊ ❊

Find Me in My Word

> *Psalm 119:97 (VOICE) Oh, how I love Your law! I fix my mind on it all day long.*

Beloved, pursue My heart. If you would know Me, you must know My Word, for it reflects My heart toward you. My longings are clearly reflected page after page: that I would be your God and that you would be My people. In it you'll find example after example of My patience and grace. Seek Me there, and you will find Me.

Allow My Holy Spirit to bring revelation as you read, and meditate on it as you go about your day. Filter your thoughts and encounters through My truth, and learn more about Me. Fix your mind on My instructions, set your heart on My word, and determine how best to honor and exalt Me in all you do.

※ ※ ※

Love, Patience, and Grace

> *Colossians 3:13 (TLB) Be gentle and ready to forgive; never hold grudges. Remember, the Lord forgave you, so you must forgive others.*

Beloved, refuse to allow your frustrations to dictate your responses. Deny the fleshly indulgence of venting, and rather choose to respond in love, patience, and grace. Quietly extend forgiveness in moments where no offense was intended and truly release any feelings of annoyance, leaving no room for bitterness, hurt, or anger to take root.

Refuse to harbor ill will. Operate from a place of love and peace with an expectation of good and a heavy measure of kindness and forbearance. Choose to be like Me. You are My child, made in My image. Reflect My character that others may know Me by knowing you. Let your walk be your testimony as you walk in grace, patience, and love.

> *Proverbs 29:11 (GW) A fool expresses all his emotions, but a wise person controls them.*

❖ ❖ ❖

Trust Me to Know You

> *Matthew 7:11 (NLT) So if you sinful people know how to give good gifts to your children, how much more will your heavenly Father give good gifts to those who ask him.*

Beloved, I love to lavish My children with good gifts. I AM YHVH Bore, the Lord your Creator. I know how I've made you and the details of how I've wired you. I know your desires and the things that bring you joy. I know you even better than you know yourself. Trust that I know what will fulfill you.

Yield to Me. Ask Me for the good gifts I would have you have rather than persistently petitioning your wants. There will definitely be times when those two things align, but I see things from a vantage point you don't (and indeed cannot), so there are things I know will bless you beyond measure that are not even in your purview.

Trust Me and trust My heart for you. I AM, and I AM the rewarder of those who diligently seek Me. Open your hands and heart to receive the blessings and gifts I have for you.

> *Hebrews 11:6 (NKJV) But without faith it is impossible to please Him, for he who comes to God must believe that He is, and that He is a rewarder of those who diligently seek Him.*

※ ※ ※

Remain Singular in Focus

> *1 Corinthians 12:4 (NLT) There are different kinds of spiritual gifts, but the same Spirit is the source of them all.*

Beloved, I AM the source, the giver of good gifts, and the endower of spiritual gifts. I created you for a call and with a purpose, and the plans I have for you are good plans - ones that honor Me and expand the Kingdom. Be satisfied with your piece of My plan, and walk it out with excellence. Remain singular in focus – eyes on Me, heart aligned with My plans and My Kingdom.

Refuse the temptation to wish you were created or called differently. In the Kingdom, every person is cherished, every gift is vital, and each role necessary to complete that which I have planned. Refuse to judge through human eyes. Be firm in having a Kingdom mentality where the goal is simply making Me known and expanding the Kingdom.

> *1 Corinthians 12:4-6 (GW) There are different spiritual gifts, but the same Spirit gives them. There are different ways of serving, and yet the same Lord is served. There are different types of work to do, but the same God produces every gift in every person.*

❊ ❊ ❊

Rest in the Knowledge You are Mine

> *Isaiah 43:1 (TLB) But now the Lord who created you, O Israel, says: Don't be afraid, for I have ransomed you; I have called you by name; you are mine.*

Beloved, can you hear Me calling you? Your name on My lips - sweet as honey and precious to Me. You are Mine. I have called you My own. I have ransomed you. The price has already been paid. Let your heart rejoice in the grace extended to you. Revel in it, beloved, for My mercy is a gift - an extension of My great love for you.

My perfect love leaves no room for fear. When you truly know Me, you know I fiercely love My children and jealously guard them. I stay close in times of trouble, and comfort in times of mourning.

I will never leave you. I created you for My pleasure, beloved, and you do please Me. Rest in the knowledge that you are Mine.

❊ ❊ ❊

Your Piece in My Intentional Design

1 Corinthians 12:18 (GW) So God put each and every part of the body together as he wanted it.

Beloved, no detail escapes My notice. I AM intricate with My design. Each gifting given with intention. Each calling bestowed with purpose. What I have planned for you is not too big or too small, nor does it matter how it compares with My plan for anyone else. Each piece is vital. Every person important. The primary aim is each person's heart and obedience to Me, and secondarily their love for each other.

Gifts are given for the purpose of expanding the Kingdom. Their purpose is corporate, not for the building up of the one who possesses it. Refuse to allow pride. Resist the temptation to judge with human eyes, remembering I AM one who leaves the 99 to chase the one.

Each detail – each gift – is important because I have designed each one with a purpose. If you reach hundreds through your flesh, but miss the one I created you to reach because you judged with human eyes rather than yielding to My plan, you will not have succeeded. Be intentional about fulfilling your part of the greater plan - My plan.

The full picture of the puzzle is only complete when every piece, regardless of size, has come into place.

So let go of any expectations, refuse to allow human judgments to encourage or discourage, and simply be intentional about yielding to Me and My plans. They are good. They are intentional. And you and your piece are key.

❊ ❊ ❊

Lose Yourself in the Ocean of My Love

> *Isaiah 43:2 (TLB) When you go through deep waters and great trouble, I will be with you. When you go through rivers of difficulty, you will not drown! When you walk through the fire of oppression, you will not be burned up—the flames will not consume you.*

Beloved, regardless of the trials you face, I AM always with you and will never leave you. The waters that feel as though they might drown you cannot rend you from My grip. Release yourself to Me and allow the water of My Spirit to saturate you with the depths of My love.

Focus on My heart for you. Refuse to be distracted by the troubles and worries on every side, for My love is larger than, grander than, bigger than anything else. Let it fill you and overwhelm you. As you're lost in the ocean of My love, everything else will pale in comparison. Allow the magnitude of all I AM to right-size everything else, for, beloved, everything is small when compared to the vastness of Me. There is nothing to fear. You will not drown nor will flames overtake you. Only the beauty of My love will overwhelm you, and that is a safe place to rest.

※ ※ ※

I AM the Righteous Judge

> *Hebrews 10:30 (AMPC) For we know Him Who said, Vengeance is Mine [retribution and the meting out of full justice rest with Me]; I will repay [I will exact the compensation], says the Lord. And again, The Lord will judge and determine and solve and settle the cause and the cases of His people.*

Beloved, I AM the righteous judge. I AM Elohim Mishpat (God of Judgment/Justice). Leave exercising judgment in My capable hands and simply focus your attentions on Me. Trust Me to know your causes and see the injustices done and to address them rightly. I see the fullness of every situation and the intentions of each heart. I understand why each choice and action is made. I know when to extend grace and when to bring correction (and how to do so most effectively). Trust My judgment.

Yielding to My judgment in no way gives a pass to those perpetrating injustice. It simply indicates your understanding that only I know how best to address each circumstance and that you trust Me to do so. Simply taking that stand is powerful warfare, for in doing so you declare that I AM trustworthy and righteous, and you acknowledge My sovereignty.

This both leads others by example and sends a powerful message to the kingdom of darkness, making you a warrior of light - beautiful and trustful of your King.

❊ ❊ ❊

Love Extravagantly

> *Colossians 3:14 (GW) Above all, be loving. This ties everything together perfectly.*

Beloved, love extravagantly. Love without reserve. Love as if you'll never get hurt. Love sees with My eyes. Love expects the best and forgives when someone falls short. Love is long-suffering, staying true beyond what logic dictates and through the ridicule and persecution of others. And love forgives those others their self-righteous judgment, choosing not to take offense and simply continuing to strive to be like Me.

Love without concern for your own heart, trusting I will heal it when it's wounded and that the moments of deep pain simply allow you an opportunity to know My heart better. True love is sacrificial, not selfish. Beloved, be known by your love. Love and love well.

❊ ❊ ❊

Walk in Bold Confidence

> *Nehemiah 8:10 (AMP)...And do not be worried, for the joy of the Lord is your strength and your stronghold.*

Beloved, stand fast in what you know to be true. Refuse to be moved by feelings of worry, guilt, or shame; they have no part of you for you are Mine - beautiful and forgiven, draped in My grace. Rejoice! And allow that joy to reassure and strengthen you. I AM with you.

I AM your stronghold and the lifter of your head (Rum Rosh). Walk in bold confidence remembering that you are a child of Mine. Let that confidence infuse others with strength as they learn and cling to their God-given identities. Believing Me and walking in My truth is a powerful weapon, for it declares that I AM trustworthy and speak truth, thus My promises are true. Indeed they are yes and amen. So again I say rejoice!

> *Nehemiah 8:10 (VOICE)...Do not grieve over your past mistakes. Let the Eternal's own joy be your protection!*

❊ ❊ ❊

Keep Your Heart Fixed on Me and Walk Well

> *Psalm 17:5 (NLT) My steps have stayed on your path; I have not wavered from following you.*

Beloved, stay fixed on Me. My desire for you to follow Me far surpasses your own, so trust that as your heart stays fixed, I will guide your steps. I will surround you with guardrails and angels - anything I need to do to help you succeed. Trust Me to lead.

But when there are moments you stumble, trust Me to snatch your feet from the net. Trust that My hand is ever extended to you for you to grab that I might pull you free. And trust that any seeming misstep will be used for good - to grow and teach you (or others). Not one thing is wasted. So keep your heart fixed on Me and walk well.

❈ ❈ ❈

Child of the Day

> *John 3:21 (VOICE) Those who abandon deceit and embrace what is true, they will enter into the light where it will be clear that all their deeds come from God.*

Beloved, walk in the light for you are a child of the day, and righteousness shines like the sun. So therefore allow your good deeds and virtuous words to shine like the Son that My Spirit might emanate from your countenance.

Reject that which is evil. Abandon that which would ensnare you, and walk in purity and truth. Be like Me and lead others by example. Cultivate humility as you choose the path of right regardless of the cost. I AM worth the price.

❈ ❈ ❈

Be a God-Pleaser

> *Proverbs 29:25 (VOICE) If you fear other people, you are walking into a dangerous trap; but if you trust in the Eternal, you will be safe.*

Beloved, refuse to fall into the trap of being caught up with what other people think. There will always be those who both approve and disapprove of your thoughts and actions, so to fall prey to the fruitless efforts of people-pleasing enslaves you and distracts you from your true calling and purpose.

Seek Me. Seek to do My will and meet My approval and pleasure. The only way to truly be safe and at peace is in My will. Be a God-pleaser. Nothing will bring you fulfillment like knowing you are right with Me. That is a place of rest and peace. Find Me there.

✻ ✻ ✻

Press On

> *1 Timothy 6:12 (NIV) Fight the good fight of the faith. Take hold of the eternal life to which you were called when you made your good confession in the presence of many witnesses.*

Beloved, stand fast in your faith regardless of the attacks launched against you. I AM with you and will never leave you or forsake you. I will not give you more than you can handle, and I always provide a means of escape. So look for it.

In that moment when you feel all is lost, remember My grace is sufficient. You have all you need because you have Me. The hosts of heaven are cheering you on and stand ready at My command. Ask Me for help for I AM here and will never leave. Refuse to allow shame or hopelessness to defeat you. The strength that you need to push through is yours already, so press on, beloved. Press on.

❋ ❋ ❋

Your Life is in My Hands

Proverbs 27:1 (ESV) Do not boast about tomorrow, for you do not know what a day may bring.

Beloved, your life is in My hands. It's fine for you to make plans as long as you hold them loosely, prepared to yield your will to Mine. You are not in control, but neither do you need to be. I AM faithful and trustworthy. The safest place you can possibly be is in the center of My will.

So resist the urge to be presumptuous in your planning, and seek My counsel on all matters. I AM the only one who knows what tomorrow holds, so ask Me for wisdom and guidance regarding each step. Trust your life in My capable hands.

❋ ❋ ❋

I AM Your Source

> *Haggai 2:8 (NLT) The silver is mine, and the gold is mine, says the LORD of Heaven's Armies.*

Beloved, I AM your source of supply. Be at peace and trust Me. Resist the urge to hold on tightly to what you have (for I cannot put anything into a closed hand) as well as the urge to be reckless or indulgent. Ask Me not just for provision, but for wisdom on what to do with what you have. Then be obedient to the instructions I give.

Strive to be content. Be thankful for all you do have rather than obsessing over the things you don't. Seek My heart rather than simply My blessing, for My heart is the true prize just as yours is the greatest gift you can give Me. Understand true value, beloved, for the trappings of this world are only temporary. Focus on that which is everlasting.

> *Psalm 37:25 (NLT) Once I was young, and now I am old. Yet I have never seen the godly abandoned or their children begging for bread.*

※ ※ ※

Rock of Ages

> *Isaiah 26:4 (AMPC) So trust in the Lord (commit yourself to Him, lean on Him, hope confidently in Him) forever; for the Lord God is an everlasting Rock [the Rock of Ages].*

Beloved, I AM the Rock of Ages - an everlasting fortress and stronghold. I AM your safety and protection, your rear guard, the One who watches over you. Put your trust in Me. Rely on Me. Deem Me trustworthy, and allow your actions to reflect that. Show the world through your bold confidence in Me that I AM who I say I AM - that I AM God.

Choose Me, beloved, without fear or second guessing. I AM the Lord of Hosts, the Everlasting Arms. I AM your rock - a very present help in times of trouble. Look to Me and know I always provide a way. Simply seek Me, and I will guide your feet and make your path sure. For you are Mine, beloved, and I do not desert My own.

❊ ❊ ❊

Obedience Born of Love

> *Matthew 5:48 (VOICE) But you are called to something higher: "Be perfect, as your Father in heaven is perfect."*

Beloved, I AM righteous just as you are called to righteousness. Being given the gift of grace in no way absolves you from the responsibility to walk in obedience. If salvation is your only motivation for obedience, then your heart is amiss.

Choose obedience out of your love for Me and out of a desire to please Me. I am well aware that you will fall short, but your desire and efforts bless My heart and set you apart from the world. Continuing to try after you've failed demonstrates a keen perseverance and sends a message to those around you that I AM worth the effort. So be a person of integrity and holiness. Be like Me.

❊ ❊ ❊

Lift Your Voice in Song

> *Colossians 3:16 (VOICE) Let the word of the Anointed One richly inhabit your lives. With all wisdom teach, counsel, and instruct one another. Sing the psalms, compose hymns and songs inspired by the Spirit, and keep on singing—sing to God from hearts full and spilling over with thankfulness.*

Beloved, lift your voice in song. I AM worthy of your praise, worthy of your affection. Release a sound. Give voice to the overflow of your heart. Let My word pour forth from your lips. Make My heart known. Release it into the atmosphere on the wings of joy. Breathe life. Prophesy.

You are created in My image, and I AM the Creator. I spoke life into existence, the sound of My voice reverberating through heaven and earth. Do likewise. Lift your voice. Don't hesitate. Refuse to allow timidity, lack of perfection, or performance anxiety to hinder you from breaking forth. I have put song in your heart. Release it, beloved.

❊ ❊ ❊

Be Insatiable for Me

> *Psalm 63:1 (VOICE) O True God, You are my God, the One whom I trust. I seek You with every fiber of my being. In this dry and weary land with no water in sight, my soul is dry and longs for You. My body aches for You, for Your presence.*

Beloved, hunger and thirst for Me. Understand I AM your true sustenance and the only one who satisfies. Long for Me as though your thirst will never be quenched. Be insatiable for Me. For though I satisfy, there is always more - new depths, new heights, fresh revelations. Continuously pursue My heart.

Refuse to settle for less. Refuse to be content with weak substitutes. Refuse to let man made visions replace downloads from My throne, for nothing compares to Me. I AM worth the pursuit. I AM worth the effort – worth building a relationship with. Nothing can satisfy you like I can. Refuse to settle for second best. Instead content yourself only with Me.

✿ ✿ ✿

Constant Communion

> *Philippians 1:4 (VOICE) My spirit is lightened with joy whenever I pray for you and I do constantly*

Beloved, keep your heart in an attitude of prayer always - in constant communion with Me. Stay tuned into My voice. Ready and awaiting My instruction. My sheep know My voice, and another's they will not follow, so trust that you will hear Me and hear Me rightly.

Freedom and refreshing are found in My presence. Be strengthened and restored with My joy. Listen intently for My still small voice directing you: "This is the way, walk ye in it." My desire for you to know My heart exceeds your desire to hear, so trust that I will make clear My thoughts when you earnestly desire to know them.

❋ ❋ ❋

An Attitude of Thanksgiving and Praise

> *Psalm 118:28 (VOICE) You are my God, and I give You thanks; You are my God, and I praise You.*

Beloved, regardless of circumstance, keep your heart toward Me in an attitude of praise and thanksgiving. There are always reasons to rejoice. Thank Me for the breath in your lungs. Thank Me for My love. Even thank Me for the blessings to come and for being constantly mindful of you. I AM worthy of your praise, and I AM worthy of your thanks.

Keeping your heart in that joyously worshipful posture positions you for more blessings while intentionally cultivating peace in your heart. Refuse to allow the enemy to steal your peace, joy, praise, or gratitude. Refuse to allow circumstances and situations to inject worry. Trust Me. Trust My love for you. Steadfastly know that My plans for you are good.

※ ※ ※

I AM the Good Shepherd

> *John 10:14 (AMP) I am the Good Shepherd, and I know [without any doubt those who are] My own and My own know Me [and have a deep, personal relationship with Me]*

Beloved, you are My precious child. You are My very own. You are a part of Me and I know you intimately. You can rely on Me and trust Me to lead and counsel you wisely, for I AM the Good Shepherd, and I care deeply for My sheep.

And My sheep know Me. They know My voice and listen (and obey) My instructions. They know My touch and follow My leadings. They choose to rest in Me - relying on Me to provide, protect, and prepare. I AM faithful and I love My little ones, not one escapes My notice. I AM good. Rely on Me.

※ ※ ※

Unfailing Love

> *John 10:11 (AMP) I am the Good Shepherd. The Good Shepherd lays down His [own] life for the sheep.*

Beloved, I love you with a sacrificial love. No cost is too great and no effort too much where you are concerned. There is no length I wouldn't go for you (nor one I haven't gone to already). You are Mine - My heart and the apple of My eye.

I have much patience for you, beloved. You need never fear that I'll grow tired of your shortcomings or lose patience with your hesitations. I know your heart intimately. I understand the whys behind every fear and failure, and I love you in the midst of them all. I remain steadfastly by your side. You will never wear Me out or exasperate Me. I AM with you and I AM for you. Place your hand in Mine, beloved, and simply follow My lead.

※ ※ ※

Be Known for Your Grace

> *1 Peter 3:9 (TLB) Don't repay evil for evil. Don't snap back at those who say unkind things about you. Instead, pray for God's help for them, for we are to be kind to others, and God will bless us for it.*

Beloved, be known for your grace. Be known for being unoffendable. Refuse to allow your pride to be pricked, but instead seek to understand the heart motives behind careless and hurtful actions, and pray for those who inflict them. You need not endure abuse, but simply remove yourself quietly rather than taking issue with your assailant. I AM the Lord and I will repay.

Be quick to forgive, leaving all to My hand of justice, for I AM the righteous judge. Beloved, bless those who curse you and pray for those who spitefully use you. Keep your heart tender, and trust Me to protect and heal you.

> *Luke 6:28 (NKJV) bless those who curse you, and pray for those who spitefully use you.*

❈ ❈ ❈

Sole Priority

> *2 Samuel 6:14 (CJB) Then David danced and spun around with abandon before Adonai, wearing a linen ritual vest.*

Beloved, refuse to let the thoughts and opinions of others cause you to stifle your words and actions. Allow the overflow of your heart to pour forth in unabashed praise. Move past simply "working through it" to a place where those thoughts and opinions no longer matter and you're not even aware of them anymore.

Be radical for Me. Be completely sold out for Me. Make Me the center of your world. Be abandoned in your praise and intensely persistent in your pursuit. Be relentless. Don't hold back. Be "even more undignified than this." Focus on pleasing Me alone. Make that your sole priority.

> *2 Samuel 6:21-22 (GW) David answered Michal, "I didn't dance in front of the slave girls but in front*

> *of the Lord. He chose me rather than your father or anyone in your father's house, and he appointed me leader of Israel, the Lord's people. I will celebrate in the Lord's presence, and I will degrade myself even more than this. Even if I am humiliated in your eyes, I will be honored by these slave girls you speak about."*

❆ ❆ ❆

Wind and Fire

> *Matthew 3:12 (DARBY) whose winnowing fan [is] in his hand, and he shall thoroughly purge his threshing-floor, and shall gather his wheat into the garner, but the chaff he will burn with fire unquenchable.*

Beloved, the wind of My Spirit shall separate the wheat from the chaff, the holy from the unholy, the pure from the profane. So that only that which is holy may remain. I AM the Refiner – a roaring fire – cleansing and purifying.

My presence begets change. You cannot help but be moved. You cannot help but step away from that which is unholy and unrighteous, for in My presence the stark contrast between darkness and light is made blindingly clear. So allow the wind of My Spirit and the fire of My presence to do their work and bring forth purity and beauty in your heart.

❆ ❆ ❆

Make Me Your Choice

> *Psalm 25:14 (VOICE) ONLY those who stand in awe of the Eternal will have intimacy with Him, and He will reveal His covenant to them.*

Beloved, go deeper. Refuse to settle for a surface level relationship with Me. See Me as I AM. Stand in reverential awe. Desperately seeking to know Me. Pursue Me as a priceless jewel. Wrestle for My blessing. Refuse to give up. Be relentless. Bare yourself to Me. Yes, I AM omniscient, but choose to share all the parts of your heart with Me. Make Me your choice.

Choose Me because I chose you. Each sliver of your heart is priceless to Me. I cannot get enough. I'm wild about you! I love to share My thoughts, mysteries, and promises with those who seek Me wholeheartedly. Let that be you. Hold nothing back, and refuse to be sidetracked or deterred. Be unshakable in your pursuit and outpouring of love for Me.

※ ※ ※

Submit Yourself to My Loving Hands

> *Jeremiah 18:4 (NIV) But the pot he was shaping from the clay was marred in his hands; so the potter formed it into another pot, shaping it as seemed best to him.*

Beloved, understand your role and understand Mine, then yield to them. Trust Me to know what is best, even when I seemingly break you. Know that I always restore. For it is better to be a vine pruned back to the stump and regrowing in strength than to limp through life injured and weakened.

Allow My work in you. Allow Me to prune, reshape, refine. Yield to the process. Refuse the urge to accuse Me of cruelty or unkindness in the moments of hardship and trial. Trust that I AM for you and I AM good. I AM always working for your best interest and the best interest of the Kingdom. Submit yourself to My loving hands.

❦ ❦ ❦

Recognize I AM a Gift

> *Psalm 37:4 (VOICE) Take great joy in the Eternal! His gifts are coming, and they are all your heart desires!*

Behold I love to give good gifts. I love to bless My children. I delight in giving them the things their hearts long for (as long as those things won't be harmful to them). But beloved, you must know that I won't allow you to lift anything in your heart higher than me. I cannot help you make idols because to do so would hurt you, and I love you far too much to permit that.

Recognize that I AM a gift – My love, My presence, and relationship with Me. Cherish this gift and take delight in it (in Me). Make Me the center of your world – your deepest joy, your heart's desire. Watch as I pour forth My blessings when you lavish your love on the Gift Giver rather than focusing on the gifts I give. Beloved, recognize Me as the greatest gift of all.

※ ※ ※

I Receive You

> *Leviticus 9:24 (NLT) Fire blazed forth from the LORD's presence and consumed the burnt offering and the fat on the altar. When the people saw this, they shouted with joy and fell face down on the ground.*

Beloved, present yourself as a living offering. You are precious to Me. Whether you feel lovely or worthy matters not. Simply offer Me you. Just as with offerings of old, I will send My fire – the fire of My Spirit – to consume the offering as a symbol of My acceptance. So know as you feel My fire, you are Mine – your life a fragrant offering before Me, pleasing and acceptable.

I will receive you, beloved. Hold nothing back. Grant to Me your whole heart. Give Me all of you, unreservedly. Refuse to allow fear of not being enough to hold you back, for I love My children, imperfections and all. You are enough when you give Me all of you. I receive you. I accept you. You are Mine.

Romans 12:1 (NIV) Therefore, I urge you, brothers and sisters, in view of God's mercy, to offer your bodies as a living sacrifice, holy and pleasing to God–this is your true and proper worship.

❊ ❊ ❊

Put Aside Any Substitute

2 Kings 23:5 (NLT) He did away with the idolatrous priests, who had been appointed by the previous kings of Judah, for they had offered sacrifices at the pagan shrines throughout Judah and even in the vicinity of Jerusalem. They had also offered sacrifices to Baal, and to the sun, the moon, the constellations, and to all the powers of the heavens.

Beloved, refuse any substitute. I AM the only true God. I AM the Lord God your Creator, the Lord of Hosts, king of Heaven and Earth. I AM sovereign. There is none like Me. Refuse to hold anything or anyone in higher esteem, for I AM the only One worthy and the only One faithful and good.

Set aside any false gods. Pause and see with new eyes that you might recognize them. Step away from those who encourage other gods or who who breed falsehood. Be true, beloved, and stand in righteousness.

Exodus 20:3 (KJV) Thou shalt have no other gods before me.

❈ ❈ ❈

Know Me in Truth

> *Matthew 7:23 (NLT) But I will reply, 'I never knew you. Get away from me, you who break God's laws.'*

Beloved, choose to know Me and know My ways. Choose to obey My instructions. I've intentionally detailed the path of righteousness in My Word so there is no room for confusion. Be mindful not to deceive yourself into thinking you can do your things your way and do them in My name.

Beloved, do not take My name in vain. Refuse to misrepresent Me – to yourself or others. Know Me in truth. Know Me by My Spirit. Intentionally align with Me and My ways that I might be able to say in that day that I know you and you are Mine.

❈ ❈ ❈

Make Love Top Priority

> *Galatians 5:14 (TLB) For the whole Law can be summed up in this one command: "Love others as you love yourself."*

Beloved, make love your top priority. Make love your first response. Be filled with My love that you might pour forth from your overflow. Be saturated by My love as you abide in My presence. Be restored, renewed, refreshed, and healed.

Choose love, refusing to indulge your pride with fleshly responses, but rather seeking to be like Me – loving without reserve, loving with no thoughts of self-preservation. Let your love change those around you. Let it be a window to My heart that they might see Me. Choose love, beloved. Choose love.

❊ ❊ ❊

Persist Until the Door Swings Wide

> *Matthew 7:7 (ESV) Ask, and it will be given to you; seek, and you will find; knock, and it will be opened to you.*

Beloved, be persistent in your pursuit. Refuse to yield to opposition or be deterred by hindrances. You know My voice. You know My heart for you. Refuse to accept anything less than My best for you. Wrestle until you come out the victor.

Refuse to turn away until the door swings wide – until victory is complete and access is granted. Do not lose heart. Trust that I AM with you, leading you, and, therefore, defeat is not an option. I AM the Lord your God, and I AM mighty to save.

> *Isaiah 22:22 (NLT) I will give him the key to the house of David–the highest position in the royal court. When he opens doors, no one will be able to close them; when he closes doors, no one will be able to open them.*

❈ ❈ ❈

You Stand with Me

> *1 Corinthians 16:9 (CJB) because a great and important door has opened for my work, and there are many people opposing me.*

Beloved, refuse to be deterred. Stay focused on the call. It is vital so refuse to back down from that which would block your path. I AM the way-maker, and I AM the key. Nothing is too hard for Me, and no force in heaven or on earth can stand against Me.

Believe what I have told you. Take Me at My word. I AM not a man that I should lie or the son of man that I should repent and change My mind. I AM steadfast and true. I AM victorious, and you stand with Me.

> *Numbers 23:19 (CJB) God is not a human who lies or a mortal who changes his mind. When he says something, he will do it; when he makes a promise, he will fulfill it.*

❈ ❈ ❈

Be Undeterred

> *Luke 18:5 (NLT) but this woman is driving me crazy. I'm going to see that she gets justice, because she is wearing me out with her constant requests!*

Beloved, refuse to be discouraged. Press on and press in. Stay focused on My promises and on Truth. Refuse to accept anything less. I AM the righteous judge, Elohim Mishpat. I will mete out justice according to My wisdom, which is perfect and righteous. Trust Me. Trust My ability to protect and provide, redeem and renew.

Be undeterred. I have given you the vision; refuse to align with anything short of what you have seen. Demand that heaven invade earth. Speak forth life. Prophesy truth. Take each thought captive that seeks to oppose My Word – both written and Spirit-breathed. My Word is truth, beloved, and I will see it to completion.

※ ※ ※

I AM YHVH Shalom

> *2 Peter 2:9 (NLT) So you see, the Lord knows how to rescue godly people from their trials, even while keeping the wicked under punishment until the day of final judgment.*

Beloved, no circumstance is so complex that I'm unable to extract you from it. There are trials I may walk you through for your character's sake, but I AM always able. So trust Me and never hesitate to ask Me for help, for I AM a very present help in times of trouble.

Take My hand and walk in peace – regardless of circumstance. I AM YHVH Shalom, the Lord your Peace, and I will never leave you or forsake you.

My joy is your strength, and it is always there for the taking because it is found in My presence. I will always receive you. No trouble is too great. No shame too heavy. Nothing will keep Me from My children nor lessen My love for them – and that means you.

❈ ❈ ❈

Be an Influence for Good

> *1 Peter 1:24 (NLT) As the Scriptures say, "People are like grass; their beauty is like a flower in the field. The grass withers and the flower fades.*

Beloved, be mindful that your time on this earth is limited. Be intentional about your use of it. Refuse to squander it or feel compelled to work without rest. Seek My wisdom on both your call and the little day-to-day details of your life, for everything that pertains to you is important to Me – both big and small.

Though each human life may be as a vapor or a wisp, the impact of each has the capability of great influence – both for good and for evil. Choose this day how you will live and the influence you would have. Exercise wisdom by knowing My Word and walking in My ways. Be an influence for good, beloved, and leave a mark on this world – one that points to Me.

❈ ❈ ❈

I AM Your True North

> *1 Peter 1:25 (TLV) But the word of the Lord endures forever." And this is the word that was proclaimed as Good News to you.*

Beloved, My Word endures forever. From everlasting to everlasting I remain. I AM steadfast and sure – unchanging and completely dependable. You can rely on Me. I AM the same yesterday, today, and forever. Those around you may disappoint and shift like sand, but I remain the same.

I AM your true north – your touch point, your anchor. Let Me be your firm foundation in a world ever changing. Fear has no place as you put your trust in Me, for I AM El Shaddai – the All-Sufficient One, and I fiercely love and protect My children. My heart towards them – towards you – is unchanging and wholly loyal. Rest in the shadow of My wings, for there you will find peace.

※ ※ ※

Grace in Persecution

> *1 Peter 2:19 (ESV) For this is a gracious thing, when, mindful of God, one endures sorrows while suffering unjustly.*

Beloved, I know and fully understand unjust suffering. I have been persecuted, accused, and ridiculed. I know well the pain of being wrongfully attacked – even by those who matter greatly to Me – and the hurt that comes with it all is well known to Me.

When you find yourself accused, judged, and wounded, remember that I have been too. Use that moment to identify with My heart. Focus on that as you choose to respond in love and gentleness, refusing to allow your pride to force you to respond rashly or in haste. Forgive those who hurt you and turn them over to My hand, trusting Me to respond as I see fit and to heal and protect your heart. Have grace in the midst of persecution, and keep your eyes on Me.

❊ ❊ ❊

May the Overflow of Your Heart Mirror Mine

> *Ephesians 4:2 (TLB) Be humble and gentle. Be patient with each other, making allowance for each other's faults because of your love.*

Beloved, see with My eyes the motivations of man. Refuse to be affronted, but rather allow the fruit of the Spirit to pour forth from you as you move in patience, grace, and forgiveness. Act in a manner in which you would have someone act towards a loved one in their moment of weakness.

Refuse to allow disunity, resentment, or anger to take root. Release any feelings of frustration, and instead allow compassion to well up from within you. May the overflow of your heart mirror Mine that others may see and know Me by your actions alone.

❊ ❊ ❊

Let Righteousness Be Your Reward

> *Luke 18:9 (VOICE) He told another parable—this one addressed to people who were confident in their self-righteousness and looked down on other people with disgust.*

Beloved, your identity is firmly rooted in Me. You have no need of posturing and, in fact, I will bring the effects of any such attempts to naught. I AM the one who gives honor. Do not try to grab it for yourself – especially at the expense of others. Rather trust Me to protect your good name.

Walk in humility. Refuse to be baited into fruitless bickering, but instead shift the atmosphere by responding in love and grace. Allow the fruit of the Spirit to pour from your life. Turn the other cheek. Remember that each time you sacrifice the desires of your flesh it is an offering before My throne, and its fragrance is exceedingly sweet to Me. Let righteousness be your reward.

❊ ❊ ❊

Season of Blessing

> *Galatians 6:7 (VOICE) Make no mistake: God can't be mocked. What you give is what you get. What you sow, you harvest.*

Beloved, have no fear, I see your humility and choice to love even when it hurts. Though you sow in tears, you will reap in joy. Refuse to believe the season of harvest will never come, for I will not be mocked. I AM a God of order, truth, and righteousness. I do not forget anything. So though you may feel as though your season of harvest is never coming, have no fear. Its arrival is assured and it will be right on time.

Refuse to allow lies from the enemy to take root and discourage you or turn your heart bitter against Me. Stand strong in faith and truth, holding fast to who you know Me to be. I AM a good and faithful God, and I will never forsake you. So anticipate your season of blessing. It is coming. Lo it is here.

※ ※ ※

Submit to Authority for My Sake

> *Romans 13:1 (VOICE) It is important that all of us submit to the authorities who have charge over us because God establishes all authority in heaven and on the earth.*

Beloved, I AM the one who lifts men up and makes them great. Position and honor come from Me, so give honor and respect to all positions of authority for My sake. Pray and ask Me to give them wisdom and help them to choose justice and mercy, but be intentional to submit in reverence to Me.

Remember you cannot see the full picture. Not understanding why someone has been given power does not give you license to thrash against it. Trust Me, honor Me, and allow My good purpose to come forth.

❧ ❧ ❧

See All My Blessings

> *Psalm 39:7 (AMP) And now, Lord, for what do I expectantly wait? My hope [my confident expectation] is in You.*

Beloved, rest assured your wait is not in vain. Though it may seem the vision tarries, it tarries not. The blessing, your promised harvest, is right on time. Await it with confident expectation. Rejoice even in this part of the journey because a multitude of blessings are found along the way.

Refuse to become focused simply on destination points, and enjoy the whole journey along with the growth and wisdom it brings. See all My blessings, not just the ones that fit your expectation of good. Wisdom and experience are blessings too. Walk with Me, beloved, and allow My perspective to shape your view.

❧ ❧ ❧

Blessed Beyond a Curse

> *Numbers 23:20 (VOICE) Look here, I received a word of blessing, and He has spoken a blessing. I cannot take it back.*

Beloved, you are blessed beyond a curse, for what I bless no man can curse. My word is Truth, and nothing and no one can stand against it. I AM sovereign, and My word will not return void. Wait upon My word. Maintain your focus on Me, and delight yourself in My presence.

Refuse to be tempted to pursue the favor of man, for My favor is steadfast and unchanging unlike the fickle favor of man. Remain true, for without fail My showers of blessings will come in due season and will saturate you beyond your ability to contain them.

※ ※ ※

Uncontainable Blessing

> *Genesis 15:5 (NET) The LORD took him outside and said, "Gaze into the sky and count the stars – if you are able to count them!" Then he said to him, "So will your descendants be."*

Beloved, My promises for you are plenteous and steadfast. Just as the rainbow is a reminder of My promises, may the stars be a reminder of the overwhelming blessings in store for those who love Me. For just as I promised Abraham more descendants than there are stars in the sky, so My promises for those who love Me are an uncontainable blessing.

Fix your gaze on Me and make Me your first choice. Throughout the ages My heart-cry remains the same: that I would be your God and that you would be My people. I hold nothing back from those who hold nothing back from Me. So delight in Me, beloved, and let your zeal be unmatched. May your passion be a flame that burns so brightly that those around you can't help but be ignited. May it serve as a lighthouse that guides the way to unfettered access to Me and the fullness of My love, which knows no bounds.

❊ ❊ ❊

May Your Motivations Be Pure

> 2 Chronicles 19:9 (NET) He commanded them: "Carry out your duties with respect for the LORD, with honesty, and with pure motives.

Beloved, I desire a true relationship with you, not one birthed of ritual or rote obligation. Be honest – not just with Me but with yourself – about what drives you. I want more than obligatory actions and feelings from you; I want your whole heart.

Give with joy. Be honest with Me about your thoughts and feelings. (I can handle messy – just read the Psalms!) May your motivations be pure and rooted in love – a desire to please Me because you love Me rather than for fear of what I will do if you don't. Trust that My heart for you is good.

❊ ❊ ❊

Refuse to Overlook the High Places

> *2 Chronicles 20:33 (AMPC) But the high places [of idolatry] were not taken away, for the people had not yet set their hearts on their fathers' God.*

Beloved, ask Me to show you the idols in your life that you simply don't see. Too often My people overlook the high places that have been in place for generations, allowing them to simply be part of the landscape. But My desire for you – My perfect will – is for them to be seen and torn down. Refuse to overlook the high places.

I AM the only One worthy of your worship, and I AM a jealous God, I have no desire to share your affections with idols. Seek your heart, beloved, and do so in truth, allowing Me to show you things you're holding above or apart from Me. I know your desire is to be single-minded towards Me, so open your heart and still your mind and be willing for Me to bring change. It is change that will heal.

❊ ❊ ❊

Vast Blessings

> *Romans 4:20-21 (TPT) ...because he was mighty in faith and convinced that God had all the power needed to fulfill his promises, Abraham glorified God!*

Beloved, will you allow Me to be glorified through you? Will you expand your faith and stand fast in

My promises? I will not love you any less if you are unable, but know that the beauty of My glory shining through your trusting heart, speaks volumes about who I AM without uttering a word.

Will you take Me at My word? Will you allow My promises to stir hope in your heart? Will you remain steadfast in your hope even when My promises seem to tarry or when circumstances look bleak? I AM worthy of your trust, beloved. Stir up your faith! Look to the stars and remind yourself that My blessings are vast and far more reaching than you will ever be able to know. Refuse to allow your blessings to be stolen through doubt and unbelief. Take Me at My word and refuse to be moved, for I AM God.

※ ※ ※

Lord God your Strength (YHVH Tsur)

> *Judges 15:14 (VOICE) When the Philistines at Lehi saw them coming, they raised a mighty shout and ran to seize Samson. At that moment, the Spirit of the Eternal came upon Samson, and he immediately had great strength. He broke free of the ropes on his arms, as if they were no more than string burned with fire, and the bonds fell from his hands.*

Beloved, I AM the Lord God your Strength, YHVH Tsur, and I will provide the strength you need in the exact moment you need it. Yield to My Spirit. Allow Me to move through you in power and might. But, beloved, never lose sight of the source of your strength.

Resist the temptation to allow pride to take root. The enemy will always try to cut you off from Me. But it is imperative you remain firmly connected. For like a cut flower may bloom for a moment, but ultimately is doomed to die because it is removed from its source, so you will wither if you do not remain deeply rooted in Me. Be nourished by My presence and strengthened by My joy.

※ ※ ※

Perpetually Faithful

> *2 Chronicles 21:7 (NET) But the LORD was unwilling to destroy David's dynasty because of the promise he had made to give David a perpetual dynasty.*

Beloved, even in the face of unrighteousness, My word and My promises are steadfast. I AM the Eternal One, the beginning and the end, and I AM relentlessly faithful. I do not promise anything lightly, for My integrity is flawless and I know what carrying out My word will entail.

Unlike men – who may justify breaking their word under extenuating circumstances – I never do. I AM perpetually faithful. When My children are unfaithful, I AM still faithful. And when their children and children's children are rebellious and pursue evil, still I remain true to the promises I have made to those who love Me. In every season and every circumstance, I AM faithful.

❊ ❊ ❊

Walk in Your True Identity

> *1 Corinthians 13:12 (TPT) For now we see but a faint reflection of riddles and mysteries as though reflected in a mirror, but one day we will see face-to-face. My understanding is incomplete now, but one day I will understand everything, just as everything about me has been fully understood.*

Beloved, I see you and know you. I have accepted you. You are My very own. I see you rightly – the true you just as I created you. Allow My vision of you to shape your own. For your own understanding is flawed and incomplete, but Mine is perfect – seeing through every intention and failure to the way you were created.

I have called you by name. Respond not just with acceptance but with fervor, for I speak truth over you, beloved, and I would have you know it and allow it to transform you into that which you have been called to be. Walk in the fullness of your true identity.

❊ ❊ ❊

Radiate Love and Life

> *1 Peter 2:1 (TLB) So get rid of your feelings of hatred. Don't just pretend to be good! Be done with*

dishonesty and jealousy and talking about others behind their backs.

Beloved, refuse to indulge in satisfying your flesh by allowing hatred, bitterness, and unforgiveness to fester nor by allowing the fruit thereof to flourish. You are children of God and of the light, and knowing and having experienced Me, you are inherently different from the world – no longer slaves to emotion.

You are no longer driven by reaction. Be one who chooses how to respond to any circumstance or situation with My heart, reflecting My character. Beloved, bear fruit. I have not promised it would be easy, but I AM with you and will never leave you. Let your godly character and the fruit of My Spirit shine like the sun for all to see. You have already been given what you need. Radiate love and life.

❊ ❊ ❊

My Choice and My Acceptance

Genesis 29:30 (VOICE) Then Jacob also slept with Rachel, and he clearly loved Rachel more than Leah...

Beloved, man's choice and My choice often don't align. Refuse to look to the acceptance of man to gauge your worth. Focus on Me and receive My attentions. Allow My fervor and favor to feed your heart and shape your understanding of who you are, for you are loved more deeply than you can begin to know.

Man does not see or judge as I do. My judgment is perfect. My approval is all you need. Honor and favor come from Me alone. Refuse the temptation to court the fickle favor of man for it will come and go – changing like a breeze – but Mine is steadfast forevermore.

> *Genesis 25:28 (VOICE) Esau was Isaac's favorite because he was fond of good meat, but Jacob was Rebekah's favorite.*

❉ ❉ ❉

Pursue Me and Hold Nothing Back

> *Psalm 25:14 (TPT) There's a private place reserved for the lovers of God, where they sit near him and receive the revelation-secrets of his promises.*

Beloved, press in. Refuse to settle for less than My perfect will for your life. Go all out. Excel at being a lover of God. Lavish Me with your time and affections. Hold nothing back. You determine the closeness of our relationship because My pursuit of you is limitless. But you must choose your part.

The difference between a shallow acquaintance and a fervent relationship is significant. Would you rather be dwelling in My Holy of Holies or wandering the outer court? How much do you truly want to know Me? Do you share your intimate secrets with acquaintances or close friends? You are made in My image, beloved. Pursue Me as you desire to be pursued. I AM worth it.

❊ ❊ ❊

Unquenchable Thirst for You

> *Psalm 45:11 (VOICE) Because the king yearns for your beauty, humble yourself before him, for he is now your lord.*

Beloved, My eyes are fixed on you, I cannot get enough. My thirst for you is unquenchable. I will never grow tired of you or find you commonplace or dull. You are magnificent. My pearl of great price. The apple of My eye. The center of My world.

You are never a bother or an inconvenience. Everything that matters to you, matters to Me because YOU matter to Me. You are irreplaceable, priceless, My heart's desire. I cannot get enough. There's no need to temper your thoughts or affections, I want it all. I long for you in a way that will never be sated. You are everything to Me.

❊ ❊ ❊

Meditate on My Word

> *Psalm 119:18 (TPT) Open my eyes to see the miracle-wonders hidden in your word.*

Beloved, ask Me to open your eyes to the glory of who I AM. Ask Me to bring deep revelation through My word. Desire to see and know. Crave to hear and understand. Then taste and see the beauty of all I AM.

If you would know Me, meditate on My Word, beloved. My heart and My ways are embedded on each page. Pursue Me. Allow My heart as revealed through My Word to change and mold you, making you more like Me.

✢ ✢ ✢

Immerse Yourself in Me

> *John 17:17 (VOICE) Immerse them in the truth, the truth Your voice speaks.*

Beloved, saturate yourself in My word. In the same way you get to know people in your life by spending time with them, you will come to know Me with greater understanding the more time you spend with Me and in My Word.

Listen for My voice. Be slow to speak, for I know your heart. So be intentional to pause and be still. Wait on Me. Abide with Me. Dwell in My presence. I AM with you always. Be intentional to tune in to My frequency. Immerse Yourself in Me.

✢ ✢ ✢

Tested and Found True

> *Psalm 12:6 (TPT) For every word God speaks is sure and every promise pure. His truth is tested, found to be flawless, and ever faithful. It's as pure as silver refined seven times in a crucible of clay.*

Beloved, I never waver. I never stumble or fall. I AM steadfast, fully believable and completely trustworthy. You are safe in My hands. Release control to Me, knowing that I love you and always have your best interests at heart. Rely on Me.

Refuse to lose heart when things don't look as you think they should look. Remind yourself of who I AM – the Faithful One – and stay firmly rooted in faith. Yielded to My plans, for they are good. My promises are yes and amen, so certain are they of coming to pass. I have been tested and found true. Rest in the surety of Me.

> *Luke 1:37 (TPT) Not one promise from God is empty of power, for nothing is impossible with God!*

❋ ❋ ❋

Choose Humility and Love

> *Proverbs 3:34 (NLT) The LORD mocks the mockers but is gracious to the humble.*

Beloved, choose this day how you would live. Will you choose to walk in sarcasm and mockery? Or will you walk in compassion and humility? Be intentional in your choice. Then walk in the fruit thereof.

I extend My grace to those who choose humility and love. For they are the ones who have chosen to walk in My image. Expect My grace. Expect My favor. I see your choice to die to your flesh and to extend grace to others in a moment that costs you your pride. Your actions bless and honor Me. I will repay.

※ ※ ※

Ignite the World

> *Romans 12:11 (VOICE) Do not slack in your faithfulness and hard work. Let your spirit be on fire, bubbling up and boiling over, as you serve the Lord.*

Beloved, ignite the world with your zealous love of Me. May your passion burn so brightly that those surrounding you cannot help but catch fire. When your personal walk with Me is genuine, sincere, steadfast, and intimate – when by observation others can clearly see your love, honor, obedience, and integrity – you will win lives without a word.

Focus on your own walk with Me and the integrity of your own actions. Be intentional to obey My voice, whether heard in My Word or Spirit-breathed. Refuse to be caught up in judging others and telling them how they should live. Lead by example and love without restraint. In doing so, you cannot help but ignite the world.

❊ ❊ ❊

Remind Yourself of My Faithfulness

> *Genesis 9:13 (TLB) I have placed my rainbow in the clouds as a sign of my promise until the end of time, to you and to all the earth.*

Beloved, I AM the Alpha and Omega, the Beginning and the End. I AM everlasting and completely faithful. That which I have said will be accomplished as surely as the sun will rise on the morrow. I AM steadfast.

Encourage yourself in the knowledge of who I AM. Stir up your faith and remember that I AM true. Look to the sky, and allow My rainbow to remind you that I have promised and will always make good on My promises. Remind yourself of My faithfulness and keep your heart true.

> *Deuteronomy 7:9 (AMP) Therefore know [without any doubt] and understand that the Lord your God, He is God, the faithful God, who is keeping His covenant and His [steadfast] lovingkindness to a thousand generations with those who love Him and keep His commandments;*

❊ ❊ ❊

The Key is to Call

> *Jeremiah 33:3 (The Message) 'Call to me and I will answer you. I'll tell you marvelous and wondrous things that you could never figure out on your own.'*

Beloved, the key is to call. Too many desire intimacy with Me, but don't pursue Me. Too many long to share in My mysteries, yet never even ask. Resist the urge to leave the pursuit to Me. Ask, seek, and knock, for the door will be opened.

Make time for Me. Make space in your life and quiet your heart. Listen for My voice. You will have trouble hearing if you are forever speaking, so be intentional about being quiet. Then trust My voice. Trust that it's My voice you hear and that I can correct you if you are led astray. Keep your heart set on Me, and refuse to allow your focus to be drawn away. I AM worth your attention, beloved, and I have so much I long to share.

❖ ❖ ❖

True Love Endures

> *1 Corinthians 13:4-8 (TPT) Love is large and incredibly patient...*

Beloved, love is bigger than you know. It is able to withstand trials and the fires of disappointment. It stands fast in the face of hardship and even betrayal. Love is a choice. Love reflects My heart.

Will you choose to be like Me – love like Me – even in the face of adversity? Will you love patiently in the face of intentional wounding? Be My hands and feet. Love unconditionally. Love is an action, not a feeling that is fickle and changes based on circumstance. True love endures.

> *1 Corinthians 13:4-8 (TPT) Love is large and incredibly patient. Love is gentle and consistently kind to all. It refuses to be jealous when blessing comes to someone else. Love does not brag about one's achievements nor inflate its own importance. Love does not traffic in shame and disrespect, nor selfishly seek its own honor. Love is not easily irritated or quick to take offense. Love joyfully celebrates honesty and finds no delight in what is wrong. Love is a safe place of shelter, for it never stops believing the best for others. Love never takes failure as defeat, for it never gives up. Love never stops loving. It extends beyond the gift of prophecy, which eventually fades away. It is more enduring than tongues, which will one day fall silent. Love remains long after words of knowledge are forgotten.*

Note: this is the first time I've felt lead to include a disclaimer of sorts, but I sensed His nudge to do so. Loving unconditionally does not have to be done up close. If someone is physically harming you, love does not mandate staying and enduring that abuse, but rather refusing to accept that their behavior constitutes who they are and how they were made – refusing to believe they are without value, and continuing to pray for them. None of those things require being in harm's way. I trust Father will give you specific instructions for your situation, and I pray for His peace to reign in your heart.

❈ ❈ ❈

Passionately Pursue

> *1 Corinthians 12:31 (TPT) But you should all constantly boil over with passion in seeking the higher gifts. And now I will show you a superior way to live that is beyond comparison!*

Beloved, passionately pursue Me. Passionately pursue My gifts and the fruits of My Spirit. Refuse to settle for a lackluster, mediocre relationship with Me. What I have for you is rich and deep. It is powerful and sweet. It is life-changing, and it is worth fighting for – worth pursuing.

Don't waste time or focus on being envious of others' walks with Me because each is unique and special just as each person is unique and special. I meet each of you exactly where you need. You don't need – nor should you want – a duplicate of what someone else has, but rather something uniquely wonderful, tailor-made just for you. That is a superior way to live. It is beyond comparison.

❈ ❈ ❈

Be My Love with Skin On

> *1 Corinthians 13:4-8 (TPT) …Love is gentle and consistently kind to all…*

Beloved, refuse to allow pride (or any fleshly response) to bait you into responding rashly or causing hurt to another. A fool vents his emotions, and you are no fool. You are master of your emotions (for My Spirit empowers you) and have no need to thrust them on someone else for a moment's pleasure.

Bring those feelings to Me. Bring all the hurts and frustrations, all the injustices and woundings. I AM the healer and restorer, I will tend your heart. So be intentional about reflecting Mine.

Walk in kindness and compassion. See past someone's poor response to the heart of why they're reacting the way they are. Are they immature? Demonstrate good behavior. Are they having a bad day? Encourage them. Are they frazzled and on edge? Seek to bring peace. Use the discernment of My Spirit, beloved, and be My love with skin on.

> *Proverbs 29:11 (NKJV) A fool vents all his feelings, But a wise [man] holds them back.*

> *1 Corinthians 13:4-8 (TPT) Love is large and incredibly patient. Love is gentle and consistently kind to all. It refuses to be jealous when blessing comes to someone else. Love does not brag about one's achievements nor inflate its own importance. Love does not traffic in shame and disrespect, nor selfishly seek its own honor. Love is not easily irritated or quick to take offense. Love joyfully celebrates honesty and finds no delight in what is wrong. Love is a safe place of shelter, for it never stops believing the best for others. Love never takes failure as defeat, for it never gives up. Love never stops loving. It extends beyond the gift of prophecy,*

which eventually fades away. It is more enduring than tongues, which will one day fall silent. Love remains long after words of knowledge are forgotten.

❈ ❈ ❈

An Audience of One

Galatians 1:10 (VOICE) Do you think I care about the approval of men or about the approval of God? Do you think I am on a mission to please people? If I am still spinning my wheels trying to please men, then there is no way I can be a servant of the Anointed One, the Liberating King.

Beloved, be free from the desire for the approval of man. For if you are driven by their fickle opinions, your goal will be an ever moving target. If you allow their praise to build you, remember that in due season you will deal with their criticism, which often is unfounded and rooted in wrong motives. I AM the only righteous judge. Would you give them such power over you?

Longing for their praise gives them far more influence in your life than is right or good for your heart. Focus your energy on being a God-pleaser. Play to an audience of One. Allow My praise and judgment to guide your actions, for My expectations are made clear in My Word and you have the support of My Spirit to walk them out. Keep your heart fixed on Me and trust Me to rightly guide you. I will not steer you wrong.

❈ ❈ ❈

Walk in Strength and Wisdom

> *Romans 6:1-2 (CJB) So then, are we to say, "Let's keep on sinning, so that there can be more grace"? Heaven forbid! How can we, who have died to sin, still live in it?*

Beloved, choose wisely and walk with wisdom in the freedom you've been gifted. Treat with sober understanding the responsibility it brings. Sobriety isn't an antithesis of joy. It merely prevents folly. To foolishly belittle the grace you've been granted dishonors and disrespects the Giver.

In holy reverence enjoy your liberty by truly being free – free from the plots of the enemy and the sins that so easily beset us. Walk in strength and wisdom, empowered by My Spirit. Reflect Me and give honor with your deeds as well as your words.

❈ ❈ ❈

Position Your Heart

> *1 Corinthians 13:4-8 (TPT) Love…refuses to be jealous when blessing comes to someone else…*

Beloved, resist the temptation to resent when someone else receives the blessing you desire, or to question Me regarding My decision on when and to whom to grant it. Trusting Me to know best and rejoicing with all in their seasons of blessing positions your heart to receive.

Resist the urge to feel overlooked or undervalued, beloved, for you are precious to Me. Walk in joy and gratitude. See and know that love all around you, and reflect back out to others what you yourself have received.

> *1 Corinthians 13:4-8 (TPT) Love is large and incredibly patient. Love is gentle and consistently kind to all. It refuses to be jealous when blessing comes to someone else. Love does not brag about one's achievements nor inflate its own importance. Love does not traffic in shame and disrespect, nor selfishly seek its own honor. Love is not easily irritated or quick to take offense. Love joyfully celebrates honesty and finds no delight in what is wrong. Love is a safe place of shelter, for it never stops believing the best for others. Love never takes failure as defeat, for it never gives up. Love never stops loving. It extends beyond the gift of prophecy, which eventually fades away. It is more enduring than tongues, which will one day fall silent. Love remains long after words of knowledge are forgotten.*

※ ※ ※

Reverential Awe (See Me as I AM)

> *Psalm 24:10 (TPT) You ask, "Who is this King of Glory?" He is the Lord of Victory, armed and ready for battle, the Mighty One, the invincible commander of heaven's hosts! Yes, he is the King of Glory! Pause in his presence*

Beloved, you know I love you and you've been told I call you friend. But never allow our intimacy to cause you to lose sight of who I AM. I AM the LORD, strong and mighty in battle. I AM the King of Glory and Lord of All. I AM the Lord of Hosts – the Commander of Heavenly Armies. The vast hosts of Heaven stand ready at My call. I AM sovereign.

In our intimacy, do not make Me small in your eyes – a comfortable little god you can keep in your pocket and pull out on a bad day. I AM far bigger and far greater, and I AM not one to be manipulated or controlled. I fiercely protect those I love, and I will not be mocked. See Me as I AM. Worship Me and know Me. Intentionally keep your heart in a position of reverential awe. I AM worthy.

※ ※ ※

Radiant Royalty

> *Psalm 76:4 (TPT) God, you are so resplendent and radiant! Your majesty shines from your everlasting mountain. Nothing could be compared to you in glory!*

Beloved, you are radiant royalty. A resplendent reflection of His glory. You know Whose you are. Just His name alone brings hope. In the deepness of night and the brightness of day, you shine more brightly because you are His.

Your strength is in Him. Identity is in Him. Hope is in Him. You will not stray. You know He loves you.

You walk in that deep intimacy with Him and have a steadfast knowledge of your true identity. You are a beloved child of God.

※ ※ ※

Take the Time to Notice

> *1 Corinthians 13:4-8 (TPT) …Love does not brag about one's achievements nor inflate its own importance…*

Beloved, trust Me to highlight your successes and showcase your strengths in the moments I deem right. Rather than trying to build your own esteem, focus on seeing and exposing the strengths and virtues of those around you.

Take the time to notice when others do good. Recognize My hand at work. Be quick to encourage and support those thoughts and deeds. Be intentional about building others up without thought of it being returned, but simply because it is a beautiful thing to do.

> *1 Corinthians 13:4-8 (TPT) Love is large and incredibly patient. Love is gentle and consistently kind to all. It refuses to be jealous when blessing comes to someone else. Love does not brag about one's achievements nor inflate its own importance. Love does not traffic in shame and disrespect, nor selfishly seek its own honor. Love is not easily irritated or quick to take offense. Love joyfully celebrates honesty and finds no delight in what is*

wrong. Love is a safe place of shelter, for it never stops believing the best for others. Love never takes failure as defeat, for it never gives up. Love never stops loving. It extends beyond the gift of prophecy, which eventually fades away. It is more enduring than tongues, which will one day fall silent. Love remains long after words of knowledge are forgotten.

❊ ❊ ❊

Enjoy the Sunset and Await the Dawn

Ecclesiastes 3:1 (NKJV) To everything [there is] a season, A time for every purpose under heaven:

Beloved, resist the urge to cling to a moment if I AM drawing it to a close. Trust that – though yet unknown to you – the next season will be as beautiful and needful as the last, and each in its own unique way.

Celebrate the end. Give honor to the One who ordained it. But refuse to cling to that which is complete, instead embracing the hope of what is to come. Beloved, enjoy the sunset and await the dawn. I AM the beginning and the end. I AM the bringer of life. Hope in Me.

Ecclesiastes 3:1-11 (VOICE) Teacher: For everything that happens in life —there is a season, a right time for everything under heaven: A time to be born, a time to die; a time to plant, a time to collect the harvest; A time to kill, a time to heal; a time to tear down, a time to build up; A time to cry, a time to laugh; a time to mourn, a time to dance; A time to scatter stones, a time to pile them up; a time for a warm embrace, a time for keeping your distance; A time to search, a time to give up as lost; a time to keep, a time to throw out; A time to tear apart, a time to bind together; a time to be quiet, a time to speak up; A time to love, a time to hate; a time to go to war, a time to make peace. What good comes to anyone who works so hard, all to gain a few possessions? I have seen the kinds of tasks God has given each of us to do to keep one busy, and I know God has made everything beautiful for its time...

❉ ❉ ❉

A Time to Act

Esther 4:14 (ESV) For if you keep silent at this time, relief and deliverance will rise for the Jews from another place, but you and your father's house will perish. And who knows whether you have not come to the kingdom for such a time as this?"

Beloved, there are moments to stand fast and wait on Me, and there are moments to act. It is vital to know the difference. For keeping silent and hoping I will move on your behalf when I have positioned and ordained you to move, is fruitless and deadly.

Allow My Spirit to encourage and bolster you. Allow Me to give you the strength and grace to do that which feels impossible. Beloved, nothing is impossible with Me. Refuse to sell yourself short, and recognize the impact you are able to have when you move in My flow empowered by My Spirit. I have not given you a spirit of fear, but of power…

※ ※ ※

Conduit of Blessing

> *1 Corinthians 13:4-8 (TPT) …Love does not traffic in shame…*

Beloved, nothing is gained by putting others down. Sarcasm and mockery at another's expense speaks to the character of the one whose breath carries it and the one whose amusement supports it, not the one to whom it's addressed. This is true even when it is intended in jest. You never know what will be the "last straw" for a hurting heart, so don't take a chance that it may be your words. Refuse to indulge in careless words remembering that you are held accountable for every word that leaves your mouth.

You have a choice to bless or to curse. Choose to bless. Do it consistently and do it often. Be intentional to build up, see the good, speak to the potential. Prophesy, beloved! Let your mouth be a conduit of blessing and your words a river of life. Let My living water flow forth from within you untainted and sweet. Be known by your delicious fruit that tastes like Me.

> *1 Corinthians 13:4-8 (TPT) Love is large and incredibly patient. Love is gentle and consistently kind to all. It refuses to be jealous when blessing comes to someone else. Love does not brag about*

one's achievements nor inflate its own importance. Love does not traffic in shame and disrespect, nor selfishly seek its own honor. Love is not easily irritated or quick to take offense. Love joyfully celebrates honesty and finds no delight in what is wrong. Love is a safe place of shelter, for it never stops believing the best for others. Love never takes failure as defeat, for it never gives up. Love never stops loving. It extends beyond the gift of prophecy, which eventually fades away. It is more enduring than tongues, which will one day fall silent. Love remains long after words of knowledge are forgotten.

❊ ❊ ❊

Be a Living, Breathing Testimony

Colossians 1:10 (VOICE) May their lives be a credit to You, Lord; and what's more, may they continue to delight You by doing every good work and growing in the true knowledge that comes from being close to You.

Beloved, draw near. Come close and abide. Fix your heart on Me and hold Me close, meditate on My word. Delight in Me. Make Me your filter. See everything through Me and My heart. Refuse to experience the world simply through the reactions of your flesh or be a slave to your fickle emotions. Rather be firmly rooted in Me.

May your life be a testament to Me. You are a child of the day. Shine, beloved. Reflect the Son. May the peace in your heart be the evidence of your time dwelling in My presence. Let My joy pour forth and infiltrate everything you do. Bear fruit. Give evidence of your relationship with Me. Be a living, breathing testimony.

❊ ❊ ❊

Shaped and Purified

> *Colossians 1:11 (VOICE) Strengthen them with Your infinite power, according to Your glorious might, so that they will have everything they need to hold on and endure hardship patiently and joyfully.*

Beloved, be patient and strong. Press into the joy and peace I've placed within you. I will never allow you to walk into trials you are unequipped, for and I AM always with you to guide you and give you wisdom when you will but ask.

Rejoice in trials, knowing they are the fire by which you are shaped and purified. Your character comes forth in beautiful array when you've yielded to My refining. Beloved, cling to the knowledge that though sorrow may last for the night, joy comes in the morning.

❊ ❊ ❊

Divine Connections

> *Ecclesiastes 4:9 (NLT) Two people are better off than one, for they can help each other succeed.*

Beloved, I have not called you to be alone in your walk. Look around you and see the divine connections I've placed in your life to encourage and exhort, comfort and inspire. You need one another. Be My love to one another and build each other up in Me.

Never replace Me with the people I put around you, but recognize My voice when it is carried on their lips. There is wisdom in a multitude of counsel. Allow iron to sharpen iron, beloved. Know that I desire you to be in fellowship with each other as with Me. I AM in your midst.

❊ ❊ ❊

Make Me Your Top Priority

> *Psalm 37:4 (TPT) Make God the utmost delight and pleasure of your life, and he will provide for you what you desire the most.*

Beloved, make Me your top priority, not a chore or something to check off your to-do list, but truly find joy and life in your relationship with Me. Let it be authentic. Share your deepest thoughts and hopes. Confess your deepest concerns and fears. Give them all into My capable hands.

Let the time in My presence shape and mold you. Let it inspire and encourage you. Let the hope found in the promises of My Word bolster your faith and keep your time of waiting expectant. You know that you know I will move on your behalf because I AM faithful. Hope in Me.

❊ ❊ ❊

Trust Your Times in My Hands

> *Isaiah 46:10 (VOICE) From the beginning I declare how things will end; from times long past, I tell what is yet to be, saying: "My intentions will come to pass. I will make things happen as I determine they should."*

Beloved, trust My timing. Nothing happens by accident or without My notice, and nothing is beyond My care. Regardless of the enemy's ploys, I will prevail. Trust Me at My word, for I AM faithful and I AM good.

I work all things for good, so even in the moments when you cannot see My hand, trust Me to move. Trust Me to heal. Trust Me to restore. Trust Me to work through every hurt, rejection, and pain and bring forth life. Beloved, My Word will not return void. Rather I watch over it to ensure that each and every promise comes to pass. Trust your times in My hands.

❊ ❊ ❊

Respect Everyone as You Respect Me

> *1 Corinthians 13:4-8 (TPT) …Love does not… disrespect…*

Beloved, give respect at all times in deference to Me. It honors Me when you treat the lowly, crass, or undeserving with respect. It calls to the hope I've placed within them, helping to show them who they truly are. Each person is important to Me. By treating them with respect – deserved or not – you acknowledge that truth, which has a more powerful impact than you could imagine.

When you are disrespectful, it speaks to the nature of your character, not that of the one you're addressing. So see with My eyes and operate with My heart. Call to their higher sense of right, regardless of circumstance or their response to you. Respect everyone as you respect Me.

> *1 Corinthians 13:4-8 (TPT) Love is large and incredibly patient. Love is gentle and consistently kind to all. It refuses to be jealous when blessing comes to someone else. Love does not brag about one's achievements nor inflate its own importance. Love does not traffic in shame and disrespect, nor selfishly seek its own honor. Love is not easily irritated or quick to take offense. Love joyfully celebrates honesty and finds no delight in what is wrong. Love is a safe place of shelter, for it never stops believing the best for others. Love never takes failure as defeat, for it never gives up. Love never stops loving. It extends beyond the gift of prophecy, which eventually fades away. It is more enduring than tongues, which will one day fall silent. Love remains long after words of knowledge are forgotten.*

❊ ❊ ❊

Lift One Another in My Love

> *Ecclesiastes 4:10 (GW) If one falls, the other can help his friend get up. But how tragic it is for the one who is all alone when he falls. There is no one to help him get up.*

Beloved, don't be found alone. Resist the temptation to close yourself off or to protect yourself from getting hurt by refusing to develop deep, intimate relationships. I will protect and heal your heart, and I have put people in your life to bless and challenge you, to encourage you and build you up.

Human relationships will always be imperfect because people are imperfect. Align your expectations accordingly. Look for both the blessings and the opportunities to bless. Bolster those around you. Lift one another in My love.

❊ ❊ ❊

Stay Teachable

> *Proverbs 19:20 (VOICE) Heed counsel, act on instruction, and you will become wise later in life.*

Beloved, stay teachable. Keep your heart in a position to receive. Recognize My voice regardless of the vessel I use to speak to you. Refuse to allow pride or arrogance to keep you from receiving from Me. You know I love to use the foolish things to confound the wise, so stay open. My sheep know My voice.

When given wise counsel, show wisdom by implementing it. It is not enough to simply hear and receive, beloved, you must respond and take action. From a place of both humility and confidence, move in the way I have counseled you. I will not steer you wrong, nor allow you to fall when you are seeking to obey Me in earnest. Rest in Me and respond.

❈ ❈ ❈

Be Sensitive

> *Galatians 5:22-23 (AMP) But the fruit of the Spirit [the result of His presence within us] is... gentleness...*

Beloved, there are moments to be bold, but there are also moments to be gentle. Allow My Spirit to show you the difference. Keep your flesh in check in the moments when it wants to reign free, but I'm calling you to keep it in check. Remember that you rule it, not vice versa. Allow Me to lead and trust Me as I do.

In the same way My voice both thunders and is still and small, so must you be sensitive to what the moment calls for. There are some to whom a raised voice will always equal violence, and in the same way, some view gentleness as a license to walk all over you. Trust Me to know the difference, and allow My Spirit to bring forth My fruit in your character as you stay yielded to My flow.

Proverbs 29:11 (CJB) A fool gives vent to all his feelings, but the wise, thinking of afterwards, stills them.

❊ ❊ ❊

Joyful Expectations

Philippians 1:4 (NLT) Whenever I pray, I make my requests for all of you with joy,

Beloved, be not influenced by the ebb and flow of the circumstances around you, but rather stay firmly rooted in Me and the joy found in My presence. With hope-filled persistence, bring your petitions to Me, trusting Me to hear and respond in My great wisdom (which may or may not align with your request).

I AM always good. I always hear you. Refuse to be discouraged or to allow bitterness to take root. Remain in joyful expectation, trusting fully in Me. Allow your steadfast trust to set the spiritual climate surrounding you, shifting others into that space rather than allowing people or circumstances to pull you from it. Stay faithful and persistent, and wait on Me.

❊ ❊ ❊

Identity Rooted in Truth

1 Corinthians 13:4-8 (TPT) ...Love does not... selfishly seek its own honor...

Beloved, you do not need to seek recognition for yourself nor strive to convince others of your value. Either they will get it or not, and neither is a reflection on your true value, but rather a commentary on their perception.

Who you are is rooted in truth and unchangeable, not subject to the fickle feelings of man. I AM the one who has designed you and created you for a purpose. I see every action you take. Nothing is beneath My notice. I see and I recognize even when no one else seems to, and in the end I AM all that matters. Seek My pleasure and trust My perception.

> *1 Corinthians 13:4-8 (TPT) Love is large and incredibly patient. Love is gentle and consistently kind to all. It refuses to be jealous when blessing comes to someone else. Love does not brag about one's achievements nor inflate its own importance. Love does not traffic in shame and disrespect, nor selfishly seek its own honor. Love is not easily irritated or quick to take offense. Love joyfully celebrates honesty and finds no delight in what is wrong. Love is a safe place of shelter, for it never stops believing the best for others. Love never takes failure as defeat, for it never gives up. Love never stops loving. It extends beyond the gift of prophecy, which eventually fades away. It is more enduring than tongues, which will one day fall silent. Love remains long after words of knowledge are forgotten.*

※ ※ ※

Rooted in Me

> *James 1:7 (TPT) When you are half-hearted and wavering it leaves you unstable. Can you really expect to receive anything from the Lord when you're in that condition?*

Beloved, refuse to be blown about by circumstances and emotions, instead choosing to be quietly and firmly rooted in Me. Seek My will and trust it when I give you wisdom. Step out in faith, knowing I AM faithful to guide each step. Refuse to give ear to the enemy's lies and distractions. Stay firm.

Beloved, you know My sheep know My voice and that I graciously give wisdom to all who ask, so be at peace, knowing full well I AM more than able to steer you through any storm and quiet your heart as you allow Me to. Waiting upon Me is not a place of inaction, but rather a state of readiness – being willing and yielded to go with My flow and allowing My Spirit to guide. Lay down the burden of "figuring things out" and seek Me. I AM faithful to lead, faithful to guide, and faithful to provide.

※ ※ ※

Keep My Precepts Forever Before You

> *Psalm 119:141 (VOICE) I may be insignificant to some and hated by others, but at least I do not forget Your precepts.*

Beloved, never lose sight of the basics – the foundation of your faith. It is not a simple thing to allow My Word to truly be your anchor. It takes dedication and focus over time, always keeping the main thing the main thing. Focus, beloved. Be intentional and make the time.

The gifts of My Spirit are an outpouring of relationship with Me, and knowing Me through My Word is foundational in that process. In the fun and excitement, don't lose sight of the essentials. Keep My precepts forever before you. Meditate on them day and night. Seek Me in My word, for when you seek Me there, surely you will find Me.

> *Jeremiah 15:16 (TLB) Your words are what sustain me; they are food to my hungry soul. They bring joy to my sorrowing heart and delight me. How proud I am to bear your name, O Lord.*

❊ ❊ ❊

Choose What is Right

> *Colossians 3:16 (VOICE) Let the word of the Anointed One richly inhabit your lives. With all wisdom teach, counsel, and instruct one another…*

Beloved, take the time to know My Word so that in the day your counsel is needed you might advise and instruct from a foundation of wisdom rather than opinion. Let Me shape your ideals – rather than the media and world around you. Refuse to be swayed by fear and popularity. Instead choose what is right in My eyes.

Resist the urge to impose your views, and rather lead by example, living a life that is rich with fruit and demonstrates Who I AM. Share wisdom when it is sought, and even then give more than just counsel (which demonstrates your own wisdom) and instead explain the reasoning behind it from My Word (thus helping others learn more of Me).

※ ※ ※

His Depths Know No Bounds

> *Job 36:26 (TLB) God is so great that we cannot begin to know him. No one can begin to understand eternity.*

Beloved, I AM limitless. My depths know no bounds. There is always more – always more love, always more revelation, always more wisdom, always more mysteries, always more of Me. You cannot reach the ends of Me, for I AM greater than you know. But how worthy of pursuit!

Choosing to spend your life plumbing My depths is a life well spent. Bear in mind, My love, that the journey is the point. All of those precious revelations and moments along the way may not be an ultimate destination, but they are the primary purpose. Relationships are always built in the moments. Choosing to "waste" your moments on Me is never the wrong choice.

※ ※ ※

Unending Love

> *Psalm 52:8 (TPT) But I am like a flourishing olive tree, anointed in the house of God. I trust in the unending love of God; his passion toward me is forever and ever.*

Beloved, you can never outrun My love. It knows no bounds. I AM your Creator. I knitted you together in your mother's womb. I know every detail of your heart and each nuance of your character. I know you intimately and I love you beyond measure.

There may be moments when your choices break My heart, or when I weep for the effects you bring on yourself. It is true that I will not force you to love Me nor choose to live in My presence, but there is nothing you could do or say that would cause Me to stop loving you. My love is limitless and unending.

> *Romans 8:39 (NLT) No power in the sky above or in the earth below–indeed, nothing in all creation will ever be able to separate us from the love of God that is revealed in Christ Jesus our Lord.*

❖ ❖ ❖

No Toehold

> *1 Corinthians 13:4-8 (TPT) ...Love is not easily irritated...*

Beloved, purpose to walk in humility, grace, and compassion. Let little annoyances and inconveniences roll off your back without effect. Refuse to give them credence or room to have impact.

Be so thoroughly saturated in My love that pesky things don't even annoy. Be so filled with My joy that nothing can steal it. Have your eyes so full of Me and My vision that everything else is put in proper perspective. Refuse to give a toehold for the enemy to leverage nor allow pride, thoughtlessness, or foolishness to injure any relationship.

> *1 Corinthians 13:4-8 (TPT) Love is large and incredibly patient. Love is gentle and consistently kind to all. It refuses to be jealous when blessing comes to someone else. Love does not brag about one's achievements nor inflate its own importance. Love does not traffic in shame and disrespect, nor selfishly seek its own honor. Love is not easily irritated or quick to take offense. Love joyfully celebrates honesty and finds no delight in what is wrong. Love is a safe place of shelter, for it never stops believing the best for others. Love never takes failure as defeat, for it never gives up. Love never stops loving. It extends beyond the gift of prophecy, which eventually fades away. It is more enduring than tongues, which will one day fall silent. Love remains long after words of knowledge are forgotten.*

❋ ❋ ❋

Inexhaustible Love

> *Psalm 48:9 (TPT) Lord, as we worship you in your temple, we recall over and over your kindness to us and your unending love.*

Beloved, you are not too much. You never will be. I've designed you to pour out your heart before Me in worship, to lavish your love on Me unreservedly. I can handle it and I want it. You are not too much for Me. My love for you is inexhaustible. Remember My loving-kindness, beloved. Remind yourself you are loved by Me.

Refuse to allow any missteps to cause you to feel lesser or unqualified to be Mine, for nothing can change My heart toward you. My love knows no bounds. My grace is sufficient for you. You are My beloved and firmly in My grasp. Dry your tears and trust My heart. Trust that I AM with you on this journey, and despite the twists and turns, I will bring it all to good.

❊ ❊ ❊

Receiving the Gift

> *Isaiah 53:5 (VOICE) But he was hurt because of us; he suffered so. Our wrongdoing wounded and crushed him. He endured the breaking that made us whole. The injuries he suffered became our healing.*

Beloved, My Son was born that He might die, graciously sacrificing Himself on your behalf – His love poured out for you, a selfless and perfect offering made on your behalf. The cost was high. Yet we choose it willingly because that is the depth of the love of God.

Refuse to waste the gift you've been given. Walk in the freedom that came at so dear a price. Cling to the Blood-bought healing for your body, mind, soul, and spirit. The price has been paid. There's no need to try to pay again out of a mistaken sense of guilt or shame. Don't belittle the sacrifice given out of love on your behalf. Receive the fullness of the gift.

> *Isaiah 53:2-7 (VOICE) Out of emptiness he came, like a tender shoot from rock-hard ground. He didn't look like anything or anyone of consequence— he had no physical beauty to attract our attention. So he was despised and forsaken by men, this man of suffering, grief's patient friend. As if he was a person to avoid, we looked the other way; he was despised, forsaken, and we took no notice of him. Yet it was our suffering he carried, our pain and distress, our sick-to-the-soul-ness. We just figured that God had rejected him, that God was the reason he hurt so badly. But he was hurt because of us; he suffered so. Our wrongdoing wounded and crushed him. He endured the breaking that made us whole. The injuries he suffered became our healing. We all have wandered off, like shepherdless sheep, scattered by our aimless striving and endless pursuits; The Eternal One laid on him, this silent sufferer, the sins of us all. And in the face of such oppression and suffering—silence. Not a word of protest, not a finger raised to stop it. Like a sheep to a shearing,*

like a lamb to be slaughtered, he went—oh so quietly, oh so willingly.

❋ ❋ ❋

Character Building

1 Corinthians 13:4-8 (TPT) Love is not... quick to take offense...

Beloved, I AM slow to anger and rich in mercy. My grace knows no bounds, and you were crafted in My image. Refuse to allow your flesh to mandate your responses. Refuse to indulge pride or self-righteousness. Instead be steadfast in humility, grace, and compassion, allowing the fruit of My Spirit to be manifest in your walk as you submit your character to the fiery trials of testing.

Remember, beloved, My Spirit is at work in each of you. It isn't your job to ensure that someone else learns a particular lesson. That role is Mine. Leave it to Me, knowing that if I desire your assistance, it will never be when you're operating in the flesh. So persist in dying to it daily, that the beauty of Me in you might shine brighter day after day.

1 Corinthians 13:4-8 (TPT) Love is large and incredibly patient. Love is gentle and consistently kind to all. It refuses to be jealous when blessing comes to someone else. Love does not brag about one's achievements nor inflate its own importance. Love does not traffic in shame and disrespect, nor selfishly seek its own honor. Love is not easily irritated or quick to take offense. Love joyfully celebrates honesty and finds no delight in what is wrong. Love is a safe place of shelter, for it never stops believing the best for others. Love never takes failure as defeat, for it never gives up. Love never stops loving. It extends beyond the gift of prophecy, which eventually fades away. It is more enduring than tongues, which will one day fall silent. Love remains long after words of knowledge are forgotten.

❊ ❊ ❊

Pour Out

Psalm 29:2 (NLT) Honor the LORD for the glory of his name. Worship the LORD in the splendor of his holiness.

Beloved, be holy as I AM holy. Knowing that you can fully rely on me to be set apart, unique in My divine perfection, allows you the freedom to fully rest in who I AM because it is perfect and unchanging. That reliance is beautiful and worthy of celebrating, worthy of worship. So pour it out.

Bask in the splendor of My glow, the radiance of My glory. Give honor unto My name. Pour your heart out before Me as a pleasing offering, a sweet aroma before My throne, a living sacrifice. Make this your life's ambition, to worship at My feet, to lavish love upon Me, to "waste" your life on Me. I will receive you. You are Mine.

> *Psalm 29:2 (TPT) Be in awe before his majesty. Be in awe before such power and might! Come worship wonderful Yahweh, arrayed in all his splendor, bowing in worship as he appears in all his holy beauty. Give him the honor due his name. Worship him wearing the glory-garments of your holy, priestly calling!*

※ ※ ※

Watch as I Move

> *Ephesians 1:19 (TPT) I pray that you will continually experience the immeasurable greatness of God's power made available to you through faith. Then your lives will be an advertisement of this immense power as it works through you!...*

Beloved, though I cannot be controlled or manipulated, there is power I have made available to you that is accessible through your faith. As you partner with Me, the fullness of My glory is made manifest and demonstrates the awesome working of My mighty strength. This is done that the world might know Me and the character of who I AM – My sovereignty.

So exercise your faith in accordance with My word. Be expectant of the miraculous. Intercede and ask for the assistance of the hosts of heaven. Believe because you KNOW who I AM. Then watch as I move, and testify of My goodness for I AM God.

Ephesians 1:18-19 (AMP) And [I pray] that the eyes of your heart [the very center and core of your being] may be enlightened [flooded with light by the Holy Spirit], so that you will know and cherish the hope [the divine guarantee, the confident expectation] to which He has called you, the riches of His glorious inheritance in the saints (God's people), and [so that you will begin to know] what the immeasurable and unlimited and surpassing greatness of His [active, spiritual] power is in us who believe. These are in accordance with the working of His mighty strength

❊ ❊ ❊

Come and Know Me

Psalm 16:11 (NKJV) You will show me the path of life; In Your presence [is] fullness of joy; At Your right hand [are] pleasures forevermore.

Beloved, in My presence is fullness of joy. The world would have you believe that serving Me is drudgery. Your flesh seeks to convince you that worldly entertainments are more exciting. But, beloved, those are simply fleeting counterfeits of downloads from heaven.

As with any relationship, ours is built over time. It requires commitment and dedication, but it is well worth the cost. For true contentment is found in it. Not the fruitless byproducts of the world's offerings that often leave you more empty than when you began, but deep abiding, satisfaction and wholeness that is found only in intimacy with Me.

No, I cannot be manipulated or controlled as a television is turned on and off with channels switched at will, but that which you will find in Me is the only thing that truly satisfies.

Come and know Me. Come discover Me. Put in the time and effort, recognizing it for the blessing it is – Melek Kabowd (the King of Glory) who desires your time and attention; Abba, your loving Father who desires the best for you; YHVH Bore (the Creator), the One who knows you intimately because He made you and understands every facet of your heart; Palet (your deliverer), the One who sets you free.

❊ ❊ ❊

Walk in the Fullness of Freedom

> *2 Corinthians 3:17 (ESV) Now the Lord is the Spirit, and where the Spirit of the Lord is, there is freedom.*

Beloved, refuse to remain in bondage in any area. Allow nothing to have undue hold over you and the ability to influence you beyond what it wise and good. Ask Me for wisdom to find every toehold so that each and every area of bondage can be eradicated.

The price for your freedom has already been paid. Choose to walk in the fullness of that liberty so that you might be all I've created and called you to be. Refuse to settle. Refuse to be content with mostly free – to be complacent about walking out the rest of your freedom. The cost has been paid, and, beloved, it is worth the effort.

※ ※ ※

Clothed in Strength

> *Proverbs 31:25 (NLT) She is clothed with strength and dignity, and she laughs without fear of the future.*

Beloved, allow your joy and trust in My faithfulness to bubble up and overflow. With YHVH Sabaoth (the Lord of Hosts) and the hosts of heaven on your side, you know you have nothing and no one to fear. Your future is safe in My hands.

Let the joy of victory ring. Let your strength be like the finest garments, and your gentle dignity – your steadfast honor and quiet assurance – be like lovely accessories, accentuating the beauty of your faith in Me as you stand assured with joy.

※ ※ ※

The Power of My Presence

> *Psalm 68:8 (VOICE) The whole world trembled! The sky poured down rain at the power of Your presence; even Mount Sinai trembled in Your presence, the presence of the True God, the God of Israel.*

Beloved, never underestimate the power of My presence. It causes darkness to tremble and the dead to come to life. It brings manifold change and tremendous breakthroughs. I AM God Almighty – El Gibbor, the Mighty God. My presence changes things. My presence will change you.

As you stand basking in My overwhelming love, allowing My joy to refresh and heal you, how can you not come away changed? Make the time, be intentional, and soak Me in. Allow Me to saturate you in the oil of My Spirit.

Then prepare, beloved. For the power of My presence brings forth response. It brings about action. You cannot know Me and spend time with Me and stay the same. It's not so much that a response is required as that it is inevitable.

So prepare to take new ground. Pour out your fresh oil with the knowledge that I AM always pouring back into you. Just step into My presence and be filled, heart and hands open, beloved. Receive from Me. Then go forth. Expand the Kingdom.

✽ ✽ ✽

Love as You Have Been Loved

> *1 Corinthians 13:4-8 (TPT) ...Love joyfully celebrates honesty...*

Beloved, rejoice in what is good. Celebrate integrity. Encourage those around you to walk in what pleases Me and is righteous, not out of some legalistic sense of morality or out of a sense of superiority resulting from your view of your personal behavior, but out of a desire to honor and bless Me and a desire for all to be blessed by walking in a way that aligns with My word.

Lead by example. Rather than trying to drag someone who is intent on doing wrong kicking and screaming from the shadows, simply shine your light unapologetically, and allow the beauty of its rays to draw others to its warmth. Shine, beloved. Love as you have been loved.

> *1 Corinthians 13:4-8 (TPT) Love is large and incredibly patient. Love is gentle and consistently kind to all. It refuses to be jealous when blessing comes to someone else. Love does not brag about one's achievements nor inflate its own importance. Love does not traffic in shame and disrespect, nor selfishly seek its own honor. Love is not easily irritated or quick to take offense. Love joyfully celebrates honesty and finds no delight in what is wrong. Love is a safe place of shelter, for it never stops believing the best for others. Love never takes failure as defeat, for it never gives up. Love never stops loving. It extends beyond the gift of prophecy, which eventually fades away. It is more enduring than tongues, which will one day fall silent. Love remains long after words of knowledge are forgotten.*

❊ ❊ ❊

Using the Creative Force of Your Mouth for Blessing

> *Proverbs 18:21 (AMP) Death and life are in the power of the tongue, And those who love it and indulge it will eat its fruit and bear the consequences of their words.*

Beloved, your mouth will bear fruit. The question is: what kind? Will it be bitter or sweet? Will it bring forth life or cause death? Choose wisely, beloved. Align you heart and mouth and mind with Mine. Speak the echos of My heart, and watch the beautiful life that springs forth.

Be mindful of each word. Resist the urge to indulge in careless ones. Understand the weight and responsibility of being a creative force and choosing to be a force for good by blessing.

❈ ❈ ❈

Choose Joy

> *Proverbs 17:22 (NLT) A cheerful heart is good medicine, but a broken spirit saps a person's strength.*

Beloved, choose joy, for it is not based on circumstance. It is found in My presence. It is always there for you, and it strengthens you. Literally. It builds you up and heals your heart, and it is even healing to your body.

Refuse to be tempted to feel bitterness, resentment, anger, or hopelessness. Rather shift your heart to focus on that which is good, clinging to the truth of My promises in the face of opposition and being steadfast in joy when confronted with trials.

Joy is a choice. Cling to gratitude regardless of circumstance, and shift the atmosphere with your laughter, for I AM good. That truth always remains. So, beloved, be intentional to always choose joy. It is contagious – a blessing that spreads. Be a catalyst. Choose joy.

> *Proverbs 17:22 (VOICE) A joy-filled heart is curative balm, but a broken spirit hurts all the way to the bone.*

❊ ❊ ❊

Acceptable, Good, and Perfect

> *Romans 12:2 (ESV) Do not be conformed to this world, but be transformed by the renewal of your mind, that by testing you may discern what is the will of God, what is good and acceptable and perfect.*

Beloved, refuse to be distracted from your call by things you are "able" to do. Just being capable of something, does not necessarily mean you should spend your time doing it.

Though you have the choice to spend your time in My "acceptable" will or even My "good" will, wouldn't you rather focus your time and energies on

My "perfect " will? I have beautiful things planned for you, beloved. I desire for you to walk in the fullness of them.

So refuse to be derailed by a sense of obligation, emotional blackmail, manipulation, or a desire to please man. Put your relationships in My hands, and lead by example, walking in all I have called you to and shining brightly for the world to see.

❊ ❊ ❊

Reflect the Son Brightly

> *1 Corinthians 13:4-8 (TPT) ...Love... finds no delight in what is wrong...*

Beloved, the world would have you believe that doing what is right is boring. It paints sin as lush and exciting – as experiences meant to indulge in and enjoy. But, beloved, the world doesn't have your best interests at heart nor is it accurately accounting the truth.

One could paint touching a hot stove as an exciting act of freedom, but without acknowledging the resulting burn and the painful time spent healing – weighing the momentary "positive" act of freedom against the lengthy negative – one is not revealing the full truth.

By painting sin as fun, joyous, and exciting, you draw others into the trap. Refuse to bring others into bondage or needless pain by delighting in that which is evil.

Choose instead to walk in a manner that aligns with My word knowing it is the path of light. True joy and fulfillment are there. And any hardships along that path are for your benefit, so that you may grow and be refined. You are a child of the day, so walk in the light and reflect the Son brightly.

> *1 Corinthians 13:4-8 (TPT) Love is large and incredibly patient. Love is gentle and consistently kind to all. It refuses to be jealous when blessing comes to someone else. Love does not brag about one's achievements nor inflate its own importance. Love does not traffic in shame and disrespect, nor selfishly seek its own honor. Love is not easily irritated or quick to take offense. Love joyfully celebrates honesty and finds no delight in what is wrong. Love is a safe place of shelter, for it never stops believing the best for others. Love never takes failure as defeat, for it never gives up. Love never stops loving. It extends beyond the gift of prophecy, which eventually fades away. It is more enduring than tongues, which will one day fall silent. Love remains long after words of knowledge are forgotten.*

※ ※ ※

Be Mindful of Your Priorities

> *Haggai 1:9 (GW) "You expected a lot, but you received a little. When you bring something home, I blow it away. Why?" declares the Lord of Armies. "It's because my house lies in ruins while each of you is busy working on your own house.*

Beloved, be mindful of your priorities. Be intentional about being rightly aligned with Me and My will. Refuse to succumb to the temptation to be fixated on yourself and your selfish pursuits, and instead be steadfast in pursuing the plans I have for you, for they are good. As you delight in Me, I will give you the desires of your heart. Be intentional to delight in Me.

When I bring to naught your efforts, it is not that I'm acting like a toddler throwing a tantrum because you didn't pay attention to Me first. It is because I want what is best for you; therefore, I cannot prosper that which is outside My will, but rather only that which aligns with it. So seek Me first. Focus yourself on Me. Yield to My leading, and trust Me to lead you rightly.

❈ ❈ ❈

Make Ready

> *John 16:12 (GW) "I have a lot more to tell you, but that would be too much for you now.*

Beloved, I have more to share with you than you could possibly imagine. How much I ultimately share depends in part on you and your preparedness. Will you make room for that which I would impart?

In the same way that to move furniture into your home you must prepare a space for it for it to be beneficial, so you must make room for Me and for My revelation. The place you make ready determines what comes. If you prepare only a corner of a room, enough furniture to redecorate the whole house would be overwhelming.

So prepare your heart, making time and space for Me. Prepare your mind, saturating yourself in My word. Prepare your spirit, staying tuned into my frequency and remaining firmly in My flow. Make ready, beloved, that I might share the fullness of all I have for you.

❈ ❈ ❈

Respond to Your Maker

> *John 10:27-28 (VOICE) My sheep respond as they hear My voice; I know them intimately, and they follow Me. I give them a life that is unceasing, and death will not have the last word. Nothing or no one can steal them from My hand.*

I AM still speaking today. I paid the price for your freedom and your healing. It was Our joy to do so, and My Son laid His life down willingly and without hesitation. Shrug off feelings of inadequacy and shame, and allow My truth – My Word – to mold and shape you. Respond to your Maker. My sheep know My voice, and another they will not follow.

Creation speaks My name. I AM your Creator, and I spoke you into being. The echoes of My voice resound in your heartbeats. When I speak, you cannot help but respond. Your very DNA recognizes its Maker. You must align. Your cells and organs must obey My word. I speak life over you, and everything in you MUST take action.

Refuse to give the enemy any hold over you when your freedom came at so high a cost. Trust the plan of the One who loves you, the One who created you, the One who is sovereign. I have deemed you worthy – worth the price, worth My time, worth My love, worth My effort, worthy of My grace. It is sufficient for you. Receive, beloved.

❈ ❈ ❈

Nourish Yourself Wisely

> *Amos 5:14 (AMP) Seek (long for, require) good and not evil, that you may live; And so may the Lord God of hosts be with you, Just as you have said!*

Beloved, hunger and thirst for Me and for the things of Me and the things that please Me. Seek that which is good and perfect and true – what is godly and beautiful and righteous, and what is holy, a blessing, and brings glory to My name.

Water the seed of righteousness within you. Refuse to be drawn in by things that are evil or the ways of the wicked. Have eyes to see and ears to hear that you might rightly divide the holy from the profane, the worthy from the unworthy, and the good from the evil.

Align with Me. Run your race by My side. Choose the side of victory and life. Beloved, that which you feed will grow. Would you indulge your sinful nature? Your fleshly desires? Or your spirit-man? Nourish yourself wisely. Satisfy yourself in Me.

❆ ❆ ❆

Complete in Me

> *1 Chronicles 28:20 (VOICE) Be strong, courageous, and effective. Do not fear or be dismayed. I know that the Eternal God, who is my God, is with you. He will not abandon you or forsake you until you have finished all the work for the temple of the Eternal.*

Beloved, I have not given you a spirit of fear. So when all seems like it's swirling around you, refuse to be overwhelmed. Instead press into Me, the King of Peace – shalom, the peace that wars against chaos – and allow Me to be your rest. I AM good and kind, and I love you.

Allow My light to penetrate the fog that would overwhelm you, and choose to bask in My glory. With eyes fixed on Me remind yourself that I always finish what I start and that I will strengthen you to accomplish all that you've been called to. Not one thing stolen, not one thing missing. You are complete in Me.

❆ ❆ ❆

At Work in Every Moment

Jeremiah 32:27 (VOICE) Eternal One: Look! I am the Eternal, the God of all living things. Is anything too difficult for Me?

Beloved, refuse to allow Me to be made small in your eyes. Refuse to believe the lies that I do not see or My arm is too short. I AM more than able. I AM the God of heaven and earth. I AM sovereign, God Most High. My glory is infinite. It knows no end. Remind yourself who I AM and that I AM trustworthy. Leave your life in My hands.

When you see a problem in your life, don't waste time and energy worrying over it. Instead, look to Me and ask Me for My wisdom and My course of action. Be excited to see My creative solutions. And when you think I've overlooked you or forgotten to act, remind yourself that is not like Me, and be expectant for the unexpected, knowing I AM at work in every moment.

※ ※ ※

Weightless in Him (Moments with God)

{my heart cries} I will seek You, God. I choose You. Regardless of circumstance. Regardless of the cost. I choose You because You are worth it all. You are so good and Your love exceeds my understanding.

{He responds} I will meet you, beloved. As you step out in faith, placing all your trust in Me. I will meet

you there. I AM faithful and My heart for you is true. Rest in Me.

{feeling His hand extended toward me, I look at it – so large, plenty big to handle anything that might come against me or give me cause for concern – and I place my hand in His. I feel Him gently pull me alongside Him, and the closer I get the lighter I feel until I am weightless by His side. Aligned with Him. Trusting in Him. Yielded to His lead. Resting in His loving care of me.}

> *1 Peter 5:7 (VOICE) Since God cares for you, let Him carry all your burdens and worries.*

❈ ❈ ❈

Stand in Awe, Stand in Praise

> *Psalm 44:5 (TPT) Through your glorious name and your awesome power we can push through to any victory and defeat every enemy.*

Beloved, no force is too strong for the King of Kings, the Lord of Heavenly Armies, God Almighty, the Great I AM. I AM your strength and your deliverer, the lifter of your head. Stand and praise, for My promises surround you like a shield, wholly reliable and forever true.

I AM awesome in holiness, and My glory and power fill the earth. Stand in awe of Me. For I AM mighty in power. Before Me demons will tremble and darkness must flee, and you know My name.

❈ ❈ ❈

Mirror My Love

> *1 Corinthians 13:4-8 (TPT) ...Love is a safe place of shelter...*

Beloved, love is a place of safety, a shelter in the storm. I AM your strong tower, a place of refuge for you. But you, who are made in My image, can also provide a safe haven. Allow your love to create a place for a soul-weary exhale, just as My love is doing for you. Provide a place free from judgment and criticism, a place filled with understanding and support.

Love can even speak hard truths without creating a need to be on guard because it does so from a place of humility – one that assumes the best and clearly sees the heart of who someone is and was created to be.

Cherish the safe places in your life, beloved. See them for the blessing they are, and respond in kind. Be My heart, and mirror My love.

> *1 Corinthians 13:4-8 (TPT) Love is large and incredibly patient. Love is gentle and consistently kind to all. It refuses to be jealous when blessing comes to someone else. Love does not brag about one's achievements nor inflate its own importance. Love does not traffic in shame and disrespect, nor selfishly seek its own honor. Love is not easily irritated or quick to take offense. Love joyfully celebrates honesty and finds no delight in what is wrong. Love is a safe place of shelter, for it never*

stops believing the best for others. Love never takes failure as defeat, for it never gives up. Love never stops loving. It extends beyond the gift of prophecy, which eventually fades away. It is more enduring than tongues, which will one day fall silent. Love remains long after words of knowledge are forgotten.

❊ ❊ ❊

Replace Worry with Prayer and Thanksgiving

Philippians 4:6 (NLT) Don't worry about anything; instead, pray about everything. Tell God what you need, and thank him for all he has done.

Beloved, I AM in control. You don't need to fret or worry. Release any fear, and rest in your trust of Me. Allow My love to draw you back deeper into Me, and My peace to quiet your soul while you press in for more of Me.

Keep turning your heart and mind back to Me as the cares of the world seek to distract your gaze. Only My love satisfies. Only My peace brings true rest. So with your mouth declare My goodness, and with your words share the things on your heart, and trust Me – the lover of your soul – to see to each need and concern. Cast your cares on Me and let your heart overflow with gratitude and thanksgiving fall from your lips without end.

❊ ❊ ❊

Tremble in Awe

> *Psalm 96:9 (TPT) Come worship the Lord God wearing the splendor of holiness. Let everyone wait in wonder as they tremble in awe before him.*

Beloved, tremble in awe as you gaze on My beauty – as the eyes of your heart become clear and you see Me for all I AM. I AM holy, rich in mercy – an awesome God, the great I AM. Meditate on all I AM. Let your heart be full. Be overtaken.

Set aside earth pursuits and distractions and make time to to seek Me. Choose to be holy as I AM holy. Offer yourself as a gift – a holy offering – an act of worship. I AM life-changing, life-giving, the author of hope. Being with Me changes things – changes you. The cares of the world will fall away as you see Me as I AM.

※ ※ ※

Being a Grateful Child of Mine

> *Psalm 107:8 (VOICE) May they erupt with praise and give thanks to the Eternal in honor of His loyal love And all the wonders He has performed for humankind!*

Beloved, what I have done is more than enough. That's not to say I won't do more, but it is a reminder to choose gratitude over greed, thanksgiving over longing. Choose to be content with what you have already been given.

Refuse to operate from a place of spoiled entitlement. There is a difference between standing in faithful expectation and pouting like a child because your prayers haven't yet been answered.

Choose well. Whom would you bless: someone you'd already gifted who quickly cast aside their blessing to extend their hand for more? Or someone grateful for your gift and appreciative of its blessing in their life?

You woke up this morning, that is a gift. You are breathing, that is a gift. Look around you. See and acknowledge all I've done, for I love My children. Bless Me by seeing and acknowledging the outpouring of that love by being a grateful child of Mine.

> *Psalm 107:8 (TPT) So lift your hands and thank God for his marvelous kindness and for all his miracles of mercy for those he loves.*

❉ ❉ ❉

Steadfastly Believe the Best

> *1 Corinthians 13:4-8 (TPT) ...Love...never stops believing the best for others...*

Beloved, continually believing the best of those around you in the face of evidence to the contrary doesn't make you gullible or foolish. It makes you hope-filled. Catch My vision of who each individual is and hold fast to that knowledge, refusing to be swayed into believing something different.

Align with My heart for them and operate from an expectation of that good. Prophesy and call it forth. Pray for them that it might be manifest. And through it all love them, extend grace to them, and steadfastly believe the best of them.

> *1 Corinthians 13:4-8 (TPT) Love is large and incredibly patient. Love is gentle and consistently kind to all. It refuses to be jealous when blessing comes to someone else. Love does not brag about one's achievements nor inflate its own importance. Love does not traffic in shame and disrespect, nor selfishly seek its own honor. Love is not easily irritated or quick to take offense. Love joyfully celebrates honesty and finds no delight in what is wrong. Love is a safe place of shelter, for it never stops believing the best for others. Love never takes failure as defeat, for it never gives up. Love never stops loving. It extends beyond the gift of prophecy, which eventually fades away. It is more enduring than tongues, which will one day fall silent. Love remains long after words of knowledge are forgotten.*

❊ ❊ ❊

As You Desire to Receive, Give

> *Matthew 7:12 (VOICE) This is what our Scriptures come to teach: in everything, in every circumstance, do to others as you would have them do to you.*

Beloved, extend grace where you would desire to receive it. Extend forgiveness where you would hope to receive it. Extend love where you see it is needed. Refuse to withhold the blessing it is in your power to give. Generously expect the best, assume positive intent, and listen for the motivations of the heart.

Be known for your grace. Be known for your kindness. Be known as one who is fair and loving. Allow the fruit of My Spirit to pour forth from you without hindrance, feeling no need to judge or criticize, but rather allowing My Spirit to be the One to convict and bring change. Just as you desire to receive, give.

※ ※ ※

The Glory Yet to Come

> *Haggai 2:9 (GW) This new house will be more glorious than the former, declares the Lord of Armies. And in this place I will give them peace, declares the Lord of Armies."*

Beloved, don't be disheartened by things that have gone wrong, and resist being discouraged by circumstances not to your liking. Instead maintain a sense of expectancy for what I have in store as well as gratitude for all I've done.

I have saved the best for last, so make ready for that which is to come. I AM the Lord of Hosts and nothing is beyond My reach nor will you slip through My grasp. You are My delight and My joy. Prepare for the glory yet to come.

❖ ❖ ❖

Allow Faith to Blossom

> *James 1:2-4 (VOICE) Don't run from tests and hardships, brothers and sisters. As difficult as they are, you will ultimately find joy in them; if you embrace them, your faith will blossom under pressure and teach you true patience as you endure. And true patience brought on by endurance will equip you to complete the long journey and cross the finish line —mature, complete, and wanting nothing.*

Beloved, allow your faith to blossom – to burst forth into strength and life as a chick breaks through its shell, having found the strength required to go forth and live through perseverance gained by the hardship of the immediate challenge. Press on and persevere.

Trust Me. Trust that I will be with you to strengthen and encourage you in your moments of need. Trust that I know what you can endure and what is needful for what lies ahead. I AM the beginning and the end, the Alpha and Omega. I AM always mindful of what is best for My children and for My Kingdom, and I use all things for good.

So in the moments when it feels like too much, focus your heart on Me. Allow Me to renew your strength, restore your joy, and give you peace.

Allow Me to guide you into the fullness of all you were created and called to be. Refuse to shy away from trials, instead seeing them as tests to be conquered that your faith might increase. So allow your faith to blossom, beloved, and do so with joy.

※ ※ ※

Pour Out from Your Overflow

> *Psalm 33:2 (VOICE) Worship the Eternal with your instruments, strings offering their praise; write awe-filled songs to Him on the 10-stringed harp.*

Beloved, use whatever is at your disposal to make a joyful noise. I AM less concerned with proficiency than heart, so simply pour out from your overflow the joy and worship you have for Me. May your love shine forth in words and notes so sweet unto My ear. May your praise be a fragrant offering and your worship as incense before My throne.

Make your praise glorious, worthy of the King of Kings. Like the widow's mite, your all will be enough. You and your praise will be accepted when offered with clean hands and a pure heart. Ascend the heights with Me, beloved, lost in the glory of My praise. Watch life and joy pour forth as the flame on the altar burns brightly.

> *Psalm 66:1-2 (ASV) Make a joyful noise unto God, all the earth: Sing forth the glory of his name: Make his praise glorious.*

※ ※ ※

My Wonderworking Power

> *Matthew 6:10 (VOICE) Bring about Your kingdom. Manifest Your will here on earth, as it is manifest in heaven.*

Beloved, I would that all would see and know My wonderworking power. Pray and ask for My Kingdom to come on earth as it is in heaven. Ask for the miraculous, then wait expectantly for Me to move – to manifest My glory.

What good father whose child asks for bread would give instead a stone? How much more expectant can you be of Me and the kindnesses I show My children whom I love? Wait. Trust. And without ceasing, pray.

※ ※ ※

Selah

> *Psalm 24:10 (AMP) Who is [He then] this King of glory? The Lord of hosts, He is the King of glory [who rules over all creation with His heavenly armies]. Selah.*

Beloved, pause. Stop and reflect. Truly take a moment and ponder who I AM. Ponder My glory, the works of My hands, My character and identity. It's far too easy to get caught up in the rhetoric and lose sight of who I truly am. I AM more than simply words regurgitated by well-meaning people who get so busy saying the "right" things that they've missed the point: relationship with Me.

So pause. Make room for Me to speak, make room for Me to love you, and make room for all I share and teach you to penetrate. Meditate on Me - on My words, both rhema and logos (whispered in your ear and written in My word). Slow down. Refuse to be tempted to rush this journey. Some things cannot be hurried. So pause. Ponder Me, beloved. Selah.

❊ ❊ ❊

Selah (again)

> *Psalm 24:10 (AMP) Who is [He then] this King of glory? The Lord of hosts, He is the King of glory [who rules over all creation with His heavenly armies]. Selah.*

Beloved, pause. Stop and reflect. Truly take a moment and ponder who I AM. Ponder My glory, the works of My hands, My character and identity. It's far too easy to get caught up in the rhetoric and lose sight of who I truly am. I AM more than simply words regurgitated by well-meaning people who get so busy saying the "right" things that they've missed the point: relationship with Me.

So pause. Make room for Me to speak, make room for Me to love you, and make room for all I share and teach you to penetrate. Meditate on Me - on My words, both rhema and logos (whispered in your ear and written in My word). Slow down.

Refuse to be tempted to rush this journey. Some things cannot be hurried. So pause. Ponder Me, beloved. Selah.

Note: *I find it ironic that in a year of sharing these "Prophetic Nuggets" daily via email, this particular post "accidentally" got posted (and sent out to the subscribers) twice. :) After my initial embarrassment, I realized God had this happen on purpose because He wanted to re-emphasize the need to pause.*

In scripture things are emphasized by repetition (so picture "Holy holy holy" as how we might write HOLY! Or as with Potiphar's dreams, when God gave him the dream twice.) Because we see this pattern of emphasis through repetition in scripture, I've learned to take note when I find it happening - especially in moments that are unique or unusual (as in this instance) - and then I ask Papa if He's making a point through it.

It seems that not only did He want to emphasize the need for a pause, but also highlight this pattern to some of you, perhaps because He's wanting you to take note of it in future! Hopefully it's a blessing :)

Enjoy your pause!

❊ ❊ ❊

Refuse to Give Up

> *1 Corinthians 13:4-8 (TPT) ...Love never takes failure as defeat...*

Beloved, there will be times when those you love will stumble and may even fall, refuse to accept these setbacks as permanent shifts, but rather as momentary hiccups. Press on ahead, continuing to believe and encourage others to believe – to refuse to give up, to refuse to lose hope.

Each step and every stumble will ultimately be used for good for I use all things for good. I AM a miracle-working God. Never underestimate My ability to move in a situation, circumstance, or heart. Continue to lift those you love (and even those you don't) in prayer. Ask Me to move on their behalf. Contend for the miraculous, for I AM able.

> *1 Corinthians 13:4-8 (TPT) Love is large and incredibly patient. Love is gentle and consistently kind to all. It refuses to be jealous when blessing comes to someone else. Love does not brag about one's achievements nor inflate its own importance. Love does not traffic in shame and disrespect, nor selfishly seek its own honor. Love is not easily irritated or quick to take offense. Love joyfully celebrates honesty and finds no delight in what is wrong. Love is a safe place of shelter, for it never stops believing the best for others. Love never takes failure as defeat, for it never gives up. Love never stops loving. It extends beyond the gift of prophecy, which eventually fades away. It is more enduring than tongues, which will one day fall silent. Love remains long after words of knowledge are forgotten.*

❊ ❊ ❊

No One is Beyond My Reach

> *1 Corinthians 13:4-8 (TPT) …Love…never gives up…*

Beloved, no one is beyond redemption. No one is beyond My reach. Regardless of the severity of circumstance, refuse to give up and write someone off. Always persist in prayer, steadfastly prophesying truth - My truth - over a person or situation. Nothing is too hard for Me.

Love without reserve. Love without hesitation. Love without thought of protecting your heart from disappointment. Let Me protect and heal you as you reflect My love. And in those moments when your heart feels the sting of disappointment (and sometimes that sting is a crushing blow), know you are feeling what I have felt, and seek to identify with Me and know Me more. My love will see you through.

> *1 Corinthians 13:4-8 (TPT) Love is large and incredibly patient. Love is gentle and consistently kind to all. It refuses to be jealous when blessing comes to someone else. Love does not brag about one's achievements nor inflate its own importance. Love does not traffic in shame and disrespect, nor selfishly seek its own honor. Love is not easily irritated or quick to take offense. Love joyfully celebrates honesty and finds no delight in what is wrong. Love is a safe place of shelter, for it never stops believing the best for others. Love never takes failure as defeat, for it never gives up. Love never stops loving. It extends beyond the gift of prophecy,*

which eventually fades away. It is more enduring than tongues, which will one day fall silent. Love remains long after words of knowledge are forgotten.

❦ ❦ ❦

Arm Yourself

> *Ephesians 6:13-17 (AMP) Therefore, put on the complete armor of God...And take...the sword of the Spirit, which is the Word of God.*

Beloved, arm yourself by immersing yourself in My word. How can one combat a lie - how can one even recognize it - if one does not take the time to know the truth? Without a foundation of truth, you are ill equipped to stand against the evil one, and that vulnerability is one too easily leveraged by the forces of darkness.

But when you have feasted on My word - meditating on it and allowing it to go deep within your heart - My Spirit will quicken it to your remembrance in a moment of need, as a sharp-edged sword able to separate not just truth from a lie, but even the intricacies of twisted truths. Remember, beloved, when My Son was tempted in the wilderness, the enemy quoted My word to him. It is not enough just to read, one must learn to understand – to know My heart. As you study, My Spirit will teach you. Intentionally unite in purpose allowing the breath of My Spirit to quicken My truth in your heart.

> *Ephesians 6:13-17 (AMP) Therefore, put on the complete armor of God, so that you will be able to [successfully] resist and stand your ground in the evil day [of danger], and having done everything [that the crisis demands], to stand firm [in your place, fully prepared, immovable, victorious]. So stand firm and hold your ground, having tightened the wide band of truth (personal integrity, moral courage) around your waist and having put on the breastplate of righteousness (an upright heart), and having strapped on your feet the gospel of peace in preparation [to face the enemy with firm-footed stability and the readiness produced by the good news]. Above all, lift up the [protective] shield of faith with which you can extinguish all the flaming arrows of the evil one. And take the helmet of salvation, and the sword of the Spirit, which is the Word of God.*

❉ ❉ ❉

Look Beyond Yourself

> *Proverbs 6:16-19 (VOICE) Take note, there are six things the Eternal hates; no, make it seven He abhors: Eyes that look down on others...*

Beloved, I have called you to walk in humility, not to be self-focused, but rather to put others first, and to be more conscious of their importance than of your own. Raise your eyes. Refuse to be fixated on self. Look beyond yourself, not neglecting or undervaluing yourself, but rather confident in the understanding that I AM infinitely mindful of you and your needs, and that I will take care of you as you look out for others.

> *Philippians 2:3 (TPT) Be free from pride-filled opinions, for they will only harm your cherished unity. Don't allow self-promotion to hide in your hearts, but in authentic humility put others first and view others as more important than yourselves.*
>
> *Proverbs 6:16-19 (VOICE) Take note, there are six things the Eternal hates; no, make it seven He abhors: Eyes that look down on others, a tongue that can't be trusted, hands that shed innocent blood, A heart that conceives evil plans, feet that sprint toward evil, A false witness who breathes out lies, and anyone who stirs up trouble among the faithful.*

❊ ❊ ❊

Exercise Your Self-Control

> *Galatians 5:22-23 (AMP) But the fruit of the Spirit [the result of His presence within us] is... self-control...*

Beloved, I have called you to be holy as I AM holy. The fact that you won't be able to walk out personal righteousness perfectly is no excuse not to do your best. And do it not out of a sense of burden or trying to earn your salvation (which is a gift freely given by grace), but out of a place of love and honor - seeking to do that which pleases Me and aligns with My word.

I have given you self-control and empowered you by My Holy Spirit. You are more able than you believe and more able even than you've experienced. Like a muscle that builds strength with use, self-control becomes stronger as it is exercised. So choose not to respond when provoked. And choose not to indulge your flesh when it's not beneficial. Choose to do that which is godly even when (and, in fact, especially when) it is in direct opposition to the flow of the world.

Exercise your self-control, beloved, and watch it grow and strengthen. When you do, it becomes easier to choose rightly. Even the desire to choose that which is in opposition to Me (or even that which is fruitless) diminishes and loses its draw. Remain steadfast. Lean into the Holy Spirit for strength. Extend grace to yourself when you fall short, and simply start again. Be holy, beloved, as I AM holy.

※ ※ ※

Life-Changing Love

> *1 Corinthians 13:4-8 (TPT) ...Love never stops loving...*

Beloved, I never stop loving you. Regardless of your choices, actions, thoughts and all the moments you fall short, My love remains the same. My hope for you is steadfast, and I find you inherently worthy of love no matter whether other people seem to find you so or what decisions you make.

My love for you is eternal and unconditional, and you are made in My image.

You were created not just to be loved, but to love - without reserve. You may hate choices or be disappointed in certain situations, but refuse to let your love - based on the inherent nature of each person and the way I created them - to change. Be steadfast. Hold to the truth of who I made them to be. Expect that truth to manifest itself. Prophesy it. Be relentless in prayer, and lavish love - and do so without strings or contingencies. Love like that is life-changing.

> *1 Corinthians 13:4-8 (TPT) Love is large and incredibly patient. Love is gentle and consistently kind to all. It refuses to be jealous when blessing comes to someone else. Love does not brag about one's achievements nor inflate its own importance. Love does not traffic in shame and disrespect, nor selfishly seek its own honor. Love is not easily irritated or quick to take offense. Love joyfully celebrates honesty and finds no delight in what is wrong. Love is a safe place of shelter, for it never stops believing the best for others. Love never takes failure as defeat, for it never gives up. Love never stops loving. It extends beyond the gift of prophecy, which eventually fades away. It is more enduring than tongues, which will one day fall silent. Love remains long after words of knowledge are forgotten.*

※ ※ ※

Love, the Primary Focus

> *1 Corinthians 13:4-8 (TPT) Love...extends beyond the gift of prophecy, which eventually fades away. It is more enduring than tongues, which will one day fall silent. Love remains long after words of knowledge are forgotten.*

Beloved, resist the temptation to get so caught up in the gifts of My Spirit that you forget My primary focus: love. For I so loved the world that I sent My Son. Love wins the day. Love touches hearts in a way that nothing else can. And in the end, love will remain when the gifts are no longer needed.

So focus on love. Be intentional to love. When in doubt, love. When you don't want to, still love. When it's undeserved, staunchly love. Whatever the situation, no matter how extreme, remain steadfastly in a stance of love. Be known for your love. Refuse to let it be shaken. Refuse to withhold it as a weapon or use it as a tool to manipulate. Give it freely and without reserve just as I have done for you.

> *1 Corinthians 13:4-8 (TPT) Love is large and incredibly patient. Love is gentle and consistently kind to all. It refuses to be jealous when blessing comes to someone else. Love does not brag about one's achievements nor inflate its own importance. Love does not traffic in shame and disrespect, nor selfishly seek its own honor. Love is not easily irritated or quick to take offense. Love joyfully celebrates honesty and finds no delight in what is wrong. Love is a safe place of shelter, for it never*

> *stops believing the best for others. Love never takes failure as defeat, for it never gives up. Love never stops loving. It extends beyond the gift of prophecy, which eventually fades away. It is more enduring than tongues, which will one day fall silent. Love remains long after words of knowledge are forgotten.*

❊ ❊ ❊

A Generous Heart

> *1 Timothy 5:18 (AMP) For the Scripture says, "You shall not muzzle the ox while it is treading out the grain [to keep it from eating]," and, "The worker is worthy of his wages [he deserves fair compensation]."*

Beloved, refuse the temptation to operate in a poverty mindset, constantly trying to get something for nothing. Surely you remember that the silver and gold are Mine. When you're living a lifestyle submitted to Me, you can rest in the knowledge that that which I desire you to have, I will provide for.

So rather than trying to cheapen the value I have placed on someone's work or trying to rob them of their wages, be excited about the opportunity to sow into their lives, trusting that fertile soil will bear fruit and rejoicing that you get to have some small part in it.

Be wise with whatever I've entrusted you with - be it great or small. This means being obedient to use it in the ways I direct you, not working so hard to stretch it that you're actively cheating others (whether intentionally or not). Remember that I love a cheerful giver, I love a generous heart. Refuse to have that stolen by a fear of lack. Refuse to be tempted into greed or envy, constantly desiring that which I have not provided.

Trust Me. Trust that I have reasons for what I've provided and what I have not and that those reasons have nothing to do with whether I love you or not, for that is never in question. Be thankful for what you have and find contentment there.

Rest in Me and look to Me. Trust Me to provide for your needs. Refusing to accuse Me of shortchanging you, regardless of circumstance. I AM faithful, and I love you - always. Stand fast in your conviction that I AM good.

❊ ❊ ❊

Singleminded Pursuit

Exodus 23:2 (VOICE) Even if the majority of people are doing evil, do not follow them...

Beloved, choose rightly regardless of circumstance or influence. Know My word so well that your compass is not shaken regardless of who is wandering off the path. Be steadfast in righteousness, and pray for those who have compromised themselves . For "there but for the grace of God...".

Stay in a place of humility, not judging those who've stumbled, but gently encouraging them to do right by walking steadfastly in ways that please Me. Have compassion, but don't be tempted to concede as much as one step on a path not of Me. Refuse to be swayed regardless of who has (or how many have) chosen that which displeases Me. Make My will your focus and destination, and be singleminded in that pursuit.

❊ ❊ ❊

Stones of Remembrance

> *Joshua 4:7 (GW) You should answer, 'The water of the Jordan River was cut off in front of the ark of the Lord's promise. When the ark crossed the Jordan, the river stopped flowing. These stones are a permanent reminder for the people of Israel.'"*

Beloved, there are moments worth capturing in a way that fosters remembrance – moments that bolster your faith and remind you who I AM and that I AM faithful and true. Don't lose sight of those moments or allow them to simply pass by with the emotions of that instant quickly fading and moving on. Take the time to establish a method of remembering, that you might be able to stand strong in the days of hopelessness and opposition because you know that you know I AM good.

Be intentional about acknowledging My good works and thankful for each blessing. I love to lavish good upon My children, but refuse to do so at the cost of their character. So keep your heart humble. Refuse to operate in entitlement, but rather in childlike trust. Take the time to place "stones of remembrance" so that you will always remember who I AM and how I move. I AM a good Father and I love My children.

> *Joshua 4:2-7 (VOICE) Eternal One: Summon the twelve men you chose from the people, one representing each tribe, and tell them to take twelve stones from the middle of the Jordan riverbed where the priests stand with the covenant chest. Tell them to carry these stones this day, and when the people make camp tonight, to lay them down. Joshua did just as He instructed and summoned the twelve men, who had been chosen from the Israelites to represent the twelve tribes, to give them instructions. Joshua: Go back into the Jordan riverbed to the covenant chest of the Eternal your God, and each carry a stone upon your shoulder, (twelve stones for the twelve tribes of the Israelites) so that we may build a memorial of this day. Someday when your children ask you, "Why are these stones piled up here?" you will tell them how the waters of the Jordan parted as the covenant chest of the Eternal One crossed the river, and these stones will fix that memory for the Israelites forever.*

❈ ❈ ❈

Palet, Your Deliverer

> *Psalm 32:7 (AMP) You are my hiding place; You, Lord, protect me from trouble; You surround me with songs and shouts of deliverance. Selah.*

Beloved, there is no situation so severe that I cannot rescue you. I AM Palet, the Deliverer - your very present help in times of trouble. I walk with you through the storm, and I comfort you with My presence.

Look to Me. Regardless of the turmoil surrounding you, I AM your peace, your hiding place - the One who never leaves you or forsakes you. Rest in Me. Listen for the songs I sing over you, and set your mind on Me. Trust yourself in My hands, for I AM good.

❊ ❊ ❊

I AM All You Need

> *Matthew 6:24 (The Message) You can't worship two gods at once. Loving one god, you'll end up hating the other. Adoration of one feeds contempt for the other. You can't worship God and Money both.*

Beloved, choose Me. Throughout history, My heartcry remains the same: that I would be your God and you would be My people. Refuse to give place to any idol or to hold anything in greater reverence than Me. I will not be content to share your adoration, for I AM worthy of your single-minded devotion.

Only I bring true peace. Only I bring true contentment. Only I bring true security. Refuse the temptation to look to your own provision to offer those things, remembering that even your provision comes from Me. It cannot love you nor fulfill your heart's desires any more than idols made of wood and clay. Only I AM able to bring true fulfillment.

Look to Me and refuse to look away. I AM all you need.

❊ ❊ ❊

Speak Truth

> *Proverbs 6:16-19 (VOICE) Take note, there are six things the Eternal hates; no, make it seven He abhors: ...a tongue that can't be trusted...*

Beloved, let your yes be yes and your no be no. Let your word be your bond - steadfast and reliable. Be true to your word just as I am to Mine, which I watch over to perform. You are made in My image. Rightly reflect Me. Speak truth, and do so consistently and with love.

Remember that your words bring forth life or death at your discretion. So choose life. Speak truth over those I place around you. The words of your mouth come from the overflow of your heart, so tend your heart with care, and take care to nurture others' as well.

> *Proverbs 6:16-19 (VOICE) Take note, there are six things the Eternal hates; no, make it seven He abhors: Eyes that look down on others, a tongue that can't be trusted, hands that shed innocent blood, A heart that conceives evil plans, feet that sprint toward evil, A false witness who breathes out lies, and anyone who stirs up trouble among the faithful.*

❊ ❊ ❊

The Only One Who is Worthy

> *Deuteronomy 13:4 (VOICE) Remain loyal to Him! Fear Him and obey His commands. Listen to His voice. Worship Him alone. Be fervently devoted to Him.*

Beloved, I AM worthy of your steadfast devotion. Resist the urge to lavish your time and attention on things that are of no consequence or value. Refuse to be lulled into a sense of complacency or become so engrossed in entertainment that you become numb to real life.

The thief comes to steal, kill, and destroy. Refuse to be taken down without resistance simply because you've become too lethargic to care. Ask Me to align your heart with My own, that you might know what matters and what is of no account. Beloved, waste your life on Me - the only One who is worthy. Pour yourself out like a drink offering upon My altar, wholly acceptable and highly pleasing to Me.

❈ ❈ ❈

My Ways Are Higher

> *Matthew 5:43 (TPT) "Your ancestors have also been taught 'Love your neighbors and hate the one who hates you.'*

Beloved, My ways are not the ways of the world. Nor do all the traditions of man align with My heart. Even the things taught in love by your ancestors may be rooted in falsehoods or misconceptions. My ways are higher.

Take the time to know Me directly. Be open to Me breaking the box of your expectations and understanding. Allow My Spirit to truly teach you. Beloved, call to Me, for I will answer and tell you things you did not know.

Refuse to be so stuck on what you believe is right that you close yourself off to Truth. Beloved, I will guide you with My eye. Be intent to follow where I lead even if it's uncomfortable, even if it challenges you, even if the cost is high. Trust where I lead and yield to Me.

> *Matthew 5:43-48 (TPT) "Your ancestors have also been taught 'Love your neighbors and hate the one who hates you.' However, I say to you, love your enemy, bless the one who curses you, do something wonderful for the one who hates you, and respond to the very ones who persecute you by praying for them. For that will reveal your identity as children of your heavenly Father. He is kind to all by bringing the sunrise to warm and rainfall to refresh whether a person does what is good or evil. What reward do you deserve if you only love the loveable? Don't even the tax collectors do that? How are you any different from others if you limit your kindness only to your friends? Don't even the ungodly do that? Since you are children of a perfect Father in heaven, you are to be perfect like him."*

* * *

Trust That I AM Bigger

John 15:14 (The Message) You are my friends when you do the things I command you.

Beloved, be obedient to My voice. Regardless of your maturity or lack thereof, I can work with whatever you'll give Me as you yield to My direction and follow My flow to the best of your ability, trusting Me to make up the difference.

There will be times when you don't understand, and times when you think I have "missed it" because you mistakenly thought you knew where I was headed. All that is fine and even expected, but refuse to allow it to harden your heart towards Me.

Trust Me to lead. Trust that you don't need all the details to successfully execute My plans for you. Simply be open to the next step and the next - on and on until suddenly you realize you know Me better than you thought you did because you've yielded and watched Me move, seen Me follow through, seen Me be faithful, and even seen Me have surprising and unexpected solutions.

Trust that I AM bigger than your failings, bigger than any human shortsightedness or insecurities, imperfections, or presumptions. I AM enough. Rest in Me.

❋ ❋ ❋

Burn for Me

> *Leviticus 6:13 (AMP) The fire shall be burning continually on the altar; it shall not [be allowed to] go out.*

Beloved, it is your responsibility to maintain and nurture the flame of worship in your heart. I cannot and will not attempt to force you into a place of intimacy with Me. I simply invite you in. The onus rests on you to cultivate a heart that burns for Me.

So stir up the flames, beloved. Resist the pull towards complacency, and choose instead to press in for more of Me. Refuse to settle for second best – for cheap counterfeits that will leave you unsatisfied and unfulfilled. I AM all you need. Choose to burn for Me.

※ ※ ※

Foundation of Your Faith

> *1 John 1:1 (TPT) We saw him with our very own eyes. We gazed upon him and heard him speak. Our hands actually touched him, the one who was from the beginning, the Living Expression of God.*

Beloved, My disciples testified from a place of personal experience. Your faith isn't built on fairy tales or urban legends, but on fact, truth, and experience. And though your physical eyes may not have rested on the Anointed One, His presence is clearly manifest in your life and the world around you. Therein rests your faith.

Stand fast in your belief. Refuse to be shaken by circumstance, or cast into a place of doubt by lies, arguments, and twisted truth. Know Me - in every facet - for I belong to you, beloved, just as you belong to Me.

> *1 John 1:1-7 (TPT) We saw him with our very own eyes. We gazed upon him and heard him speak. Our hands actually touched him, the one who was from the beginning, the Living Expression of God. This Life-Giver was made visible and we have seen him. We testify to this truth: the eternal Life-Giver lived face-to-face with the Father and has now dawned upon us. So we proclaim to you what we have seen and heard about this Life-Giver so that we may share and enjoy this life together. For truly our fellowship is with the Father and with his Son, Jesus, the Anointed One. We are writing these things to you because we want to release to you our fullness of joy. This is the life-giving message we heard him share and it's still ringing in our ears. We now repeat his words to you: God is pure light. You will never find even a trace of darkness in him. If we claim that we share life with him, but keep walking in the realm of darkness, we're fooling ourselves and not living the truth. But if we keep living in the pure light that surrounds him, we share unbroken fellowship with one another, and the blood of Jesus, his Son, continually cleanses us from all sin.*

❊ ❊ ❊

I Orchestrate in Harmony

> *1 Corinthians 14:32 (VOICE) ...the prophetic spirits are under the control of the prophets...*

Beloved, cultivate a sensitivity to My leading, and extend grace to yourself in the process. Trust those I've placed in leadership to direct you according to My will. Even if they are shutting down what you are sensing, know that I AM sovereign. Since I will not force Myself on anyone nor remove your natural abilities and functions, you are always able to stop or pause. I have placed you under authority, and you honor Me when you honor your superiors or those Ive placed over you. They may fall short, but leave room for them to miss Me, even as you desire that grace for yourself.

Refuse the urge to try to control Me (or them) or the need to understand everything in your natural mind, instead allowing Me to move. My Spirit empowers, moving in strength and harmony. As you yield to My Spirit, we will flow together, breathing life and operating in truth.

So remember, beloved, to yield to authority – both Mine and that of those in the natural who have been granted the role. Honor them as you would Me. Trust that they are reflecting My heart and implementing My wishes to the best of their ability, and pray for them to do so. Operate in order. Cultivate My presence. And for those tasked with facilitating My presence, trust My Spirit to lead you. I orchestrate in harmony.

> *1 Corinthians 14:31-33 (VOICE) To avoid confusion and create a space where all can learn and be encouraged, let only one prophet speak at a time without interruption. You see, the prophetic spirits are under the control of the prophets because God is the author of order, not confusion. This is how it is in all gatherings of the saints.*

※ ※ ※

Sacrifice Your Ego

> *Matthew 5:43-48 (TPT) ...I say to you, love your enemy...*

Beloved, choose not to respond as the world does. Resist the urge to indulge your flesh, and refuse to take offense or seek out retribution. Put others in My hands and simply operate in love. This doesn't mean openly and continually being exposed to abuse - for that is not My heart for you - but rather, in the moments when you're faced with adversity, respond in steadfast, life-changing love.

You never know when an unexpected response of love - a kind and gentle word - will shift someone's entire life. Be willing to pay the cost of your pride. When your identity is in Me, your fleshly ego is a price well paid to change a heart. And though you may not see the impact your love has, I do. I see it as a most beautiful and pleasing sacrifice, most acceptable in My sight.

> *Matthew 5:43-48 (TPT) "Your ancestors have also been taught 'Love your neighbors and hate the one*

who hates you.' However, I say to you, love your enemy, bless the one who curses you, do something wonderful for the one who hates you, and respond to the very ones who persecute you by praying for them. For that will reveal your identity as children of your heavenly Father. He is kind to all by bringing the sunrise to warm and rainfall to refresh whether a person does what is good or evil. What reward do you deserve if you only love the loveable? Don't even the tax collectors do that? How are you any different from others if you limit your kindness only to your friends? Don't even the ungodly do that? Since you are children of a perfect Father in heaven, you are to be perfect like him."

※ ※ ※

Be Led By My Spirit

> *1 Corinthians 14:33 (VOICE) ...God is the author of order, not confusion...*

Beloved, I AM not the author of chaos, nor do I incite discord. I do not work contrary to My goal or My word. As My children yield to My flow, they find themselves working in concert, creating a harmony that glorifies and honors their King. As you each align with your roles within the flow, beauty and life pour forth.

Trust each to be led by My Spirit (and for Me to bring correction if they're not). Trust the authority I have put in place to be a catalyst for unity and to lead and guide rightly, and pray for them to walk in the fullness of that call. Put your focus on aligning yourself with My purpose for you, and refuse to be distracted by whether or not others are doing likewise.

In the end, remember I AM sovereign. Regardless of human shortcomings, I delight to move in and through it all. Yield to Me, focus on Me, and usher in My Kingdom here on earth.

> *1 Corinthians 14:31-33 (VOICE) To avoid confusion and create a space where all can learn and be encouraged, let only one prophet speak at a time without interruption. You see, the prophetic spirits are under the control of the prophets because God is the author of order, not confusion. This is how it is in all gatherings of the saints.*

✧ ✧ ✧

Drink Deeply

> *1 John 1:1-7 (TPT) ...This Life-Giver was made visible and we have seen him...*

Beloved, I make Myself known to those who love Me. My handiwork surrounds you. Choose to have eyes that see, hearts that expect, and minds that believe. Encounter Me. Without air and water, you have no life, but beloved, I AM the life-giver. How much more vital is relationship with Me!

I AM essential. Drink deeply. Be saturated and thoroughly satisfied in My presence. Refuse to waste your efforts on that which profits nothing, choosing instead to place your focus on Me. Flourish under My loving hand.

> *1 John 1:1-7 (TPT) We saw him with our very own eyes. We gazed upon him and heard him speak. Our hands actually touched him, the one who was from the beginning, the Living Expression of God. This Life-Giver was made visible and we have seen him. We testify to this truth: the eternal Life-Giver lived face-to-face with the Father and has now dawned upon us. So we proclaim to you what we have seen and heard about this Life-Giver so that we may share and enjoy this life together. For truly our fellowship is with the Father and with his Son, Jesus, the Anointed One. We are writing these things to you because we want to release to you our fullness of joy. This is the life-giving message we heard him share and it's still ringing in our ears. We now repeat his words to you: God is pure light. You will never find even a trace of darkness in him. If we claim that we share life with him, but keep walking in the realm of darkness, we're fooling ourselves and not living the truth. But if we keep living in the pure light that surrounds him, we share unbroken fellowship with one another, and the blood of Jesus, his Son, continually cleanses us from all sin.*

※ ※ ※

Be a Fool For Me

> *1 Corinthians 12:7 (TPT) Each believer has received a gift that manifests the Spirit's power and*

presence. That gift is given for the good of the whole community.

Beloved, allow My Spirit to empower you to operate in the supernatural. I have placed gifts within you for My glory. Resist the urge to withhold them because of insecurity, doubt, or pride. Be a fool for Me. Withhold nothing. Allow My Spirit to flow like water over and through you.

Refuse to be sidetracked or derailed by comparisons or petty jealousy, I flow through each of you in a way that is unique and perfect for you. Yield to that flow, with no concerns of vanity or judgment of man, simply focus on releasing all I've empowered you to impart. Glorify Me.

1 Corinthians 12:7-12 (TPT) Each believer has received a gift that manifests the Spirit's power and presence. That gift is given for the good of the whole community. The Spirit gives one person a word of wisdom, but to the next person the same Spirit gives a word of knowledge. Another will receive the gift of faith by the same Spirit, and still another gifts of healing—all from the one Spirit. One person is enabled by the Spirit to perform miracles, another to prophesy, while another is enabled to distinguish those prophetic spirits. The next one speaks in various kinds of unknown languages, while another is able to interpret those languages. One Spirit works all these things in each of them individually as He sees fit. Just as a body is one whole made up of many different parts, and all the different parts comprise the one body, so it is with the Anointed One.

❈ ❈ ❈

I Belong to You (Moments with God)

{He whispers to my heart} I belong to you.

{He pauses, waiting for that to penetrate. As I sit trying to really "get" it, He repeats Himself} I belong to you.

{Immediately the verse in Song of Solomon (which I have in Hebrew on my ring) comes to mind} "I am my beloved's, and my beloved is mine." Such a seemingly basic message, and yet after decades of following Him, still I struggle to know it. Still I struggle to feel worthy. But He reminds me that His love has nothing to do with whether or not I am worthy. It has to do with the fact that He chose me anyway. Regardless of my human failings and imperfections, He chose me. And He chose you. May the beauty of that penetrate your heart today.

> *Song of Songs 2:16 (KJV) My beloved [is] mine, and I [am] his: he feedeth among the lilies.*

❈ ❈ ❈

Embrace Your Uniqueness

> *Psalm 139:14 (TPT) I will offer You my grateful heart, for I am Your unique creation, filled with wonder and awe. You have approached even the smallest details with excellence; Your works are wonderful; I carry this knowledge deep within my soul.*

Beloved, resist the urge to compare yourself to others, for you have been uniquely made, and if you use others as your guideposts, you will likely take yourself off track from My perfect will. Refuse to hold others up as the ideal to be achieved. Only My Son should have that honor.

Instead seek Me. Ask Me how you should live and who you should be. Beloved, your Creator knows you intimately, and I love every part of how I made you. You truly are fearfully and wonderfully made.

So own it. Embrace your unique makeup. You are a gift, created with intentionality and a purpose. Resist the urge to withhold that gift by hiding who you are. Refuse to believe the lie that different is somehow "wrong," and trust that I know what I'm doing. Beloved, you are beautiful and so loved. You are worth knowing. Shine without shame.

❉ ❉ ❉

Bless Without Reserve

> *Matthew 5:43-48 (TPT) ...bless the one who curses you...*

Beloved, refuse to retaliate in kind. Refuse to stoop to a level that diminishes your witness. Responding in love isn't the same thing as receiving the curse they've spoken. It is simply choosing a higher path - My path.

So bless all you touch, including those who curse you or seek to do you harm. Ask Me to move in their lives. Ask Me to touch them and heal their hearts. Blessing someone isn't submitting yourself as a doormat. It is refusing to shift into a negative mindset simply because someone else is doing so. Operate in love and bless without reserve.

> *Matthew 5:43-48 (TPT) "Your ancestors have also been taught 'Love your neighbors and hate the one who hates you.' However, I say to you, love your enemy, bless the one who curses you, do something wonderful for the one who hates you, and respond to the very ones who persecute you by praying for them. For that will reveal your identity as children of your heavenly Father. He is kind to all by bringing the sunrise to warm and rainfall to refresh whether a person does what is good or evil. What reward do you deserve if you only love the loveable? Don't even the tax collectors do that? How are you any different from others if you limit your kindness only to your friends? Don't even the ungodly do that? Since you are children of a perfect Father in heaven, you are to be perfect like him."*

❈ ❈ ❈

Choose to Value Life

> *Proverbs 6:16-17 (VOICE) Take note, there are six things the Eternal hates; no, make it seven He abhors...hands that shed innocent blood...*

Beloved, life comes from Me. It is a gift. Do not be quick to judge it or undervalue it. Refuse to be tempted to believe one life is more valuable than another, for all life is precious in My eyes. I love My children - My beautiful creation - each created with a purpose and a call. Regardless of the scale of the call, each is vital to the tapestry I AM weaving. So choose to value life. Seek to find and support My purpose. Choose to rest in My sovereignty, and know My purposes will remain.

> *Proverbs 6:16-19 (VOICE) Take note, there are six things the Eternal hates; no, make it seven He abhors: Eyes that look down on others, a tongue that can't be trusted, hands that shed innocent blood, A heart that conceives evil plans, feet that sprint toward evil, A false witness who breathes out lies, and anyone who stirs up trouble among the faithful.*

❊ ❊ ❊

Find Your Rest in Me

> *Matthew 11:28 (GW) "Come to me, all who are tired from carrying heavy loads, and I will give you rest.*

Beloved, refuse to be needlessly weighed down, carrying the weight of the world on your shoulders - a burden you were not intended to endure. Choose instead to trust Me. I am mindful of all the details, so place your cares and concerns in My capable hands, and trust Me to carry the load.

Find your rest in Me. Worrying is fruitless, so choose instead to be steadfast in faithful reliance on the One who loves you, who created you, and who cares for you. I AM All you need. Find your strength in Me.

> *Matthew 11:28-30 (GW) "Come to me, all who are tired from carrying heavy loads, and I will give you rest. Place my yoke over your shoulders, and learn from me, because I am gentle and humble. Then you will find rest for yourselves because my yoke is easy and my burden is light."*

❁ ❁ ❁

Trust without Expectations

> *Daniel 3:17-18 (NIV) If we are thrown into the blazing furnace, the God we serve is able to deliver us from it, and he will deliver us from Your Majesty's hand. But even if he does not, we want you to know, Your Majesty, that we will not serve your gods or worship the image of gold you have set up."*

Beloved, trust in Me and leave the outcome in My hands. Be expectant of Me without having expectations for specific results. For My ways are not your ways nor are My thoughts your thoughts, so My course of action may not make sense to you. But trust Me enough to know that even if you don't "get" it and even if it isn't what you thought or hoped, for I AM always good.

Expect Me to be good without trying to mandate what that looks like. I AM the Righteous One, the Faithful God. Trust Me to know what is best. Keep your heart in a place of gratitude and praise, and be steadfast in it. Refuse to let circumstances shake or confuse you, and simply rest in Me.

❊ ❊ ❊

Unconditional Trust

> *Matthew 26:39 (TPT) Then he walked a short distance away, and overcome with grief, he threw himself facedown on the ground and prayed, "My Father, if there is any way you can deliver me from this suffering, please take it from me. Yet what I want is not important, for I only desire to fulfill your plan for me." Then an angel from heaven appeared to strengthen him.*

Beloved, refuse to try to contain Me or to put conditions on your trust in Me. I see what you do not and am weaving a greater picture together than the piece you are in. And yet your piece is precious to Me - each of My children is so important to Me - so know that I AM working all things together for good.

As you trust Me unconditionally, I will strengthen you. I will minister to you even with My angels, for I AM keenly aware of your thoughts and needs. Put your faith in Me and leave it there. Resist the urge to put restrictions or conditions on it, and simply trust Me unconditionally.

❊ ❊ ❊

Mighty in Me

> *2 Corinthians 10:4 (NKJV) For the weapons of our warfare [are] not carnal but mighty in God for pulling down strongholds,*

Beloved, be not defenseless in the face of your enemy, but rather, having donned your armor, cling to your shield of faith and wield your sword of truth. For I have equipped you to withstand the onslaught of the enemy of your soul.

And yet, just as one would not attempt a marathon without having trained, be mindful to exercise your faith at all times to be prepared for the times of turmoil which will surely come. I AM with you to strengthen you. Do your part, for I have not left you helpless or defenseless, but mighty in Me.

※ ※ ※

The Power of My Voice

> *Psalm 29:4 (AMP) The voice of the Lord is powerful; The voice of the Lord is full of majesty.*

Beloved, My voice carries more weight than any other. My words are rooted in beauty and truth. Find time to tarry with Me. Be intentional about silencing the voices that seek to distract you from My presence and purpose.

No matter how well-meaning or well-intentioned, if words are not carried on the breath of My Spirit, they do not bring true life. So make time, find a quiet place - both externally and internally - and abide with Me. Let the power of My voice bring comfort and effect change.

※ ※ ※

I AM YHVH Shalom

> *Exodus 33:14 (TLV) "My presence will go with you, and I will give you rest," He answered.*

Beloved, you need not carry the weight of the world, or allow stresses and worries to consume you. I AM YHVH Shalom, the Lord your peace. In Me you will find rest.

Tarry with Me, beloved. For My yoke is easy and My burden light. Chaos has no foothold here. Darkness cannot remain where light has decided to dwell. I AM the Lord of the Breakthrough. Trust Me to make it so.

> *Psalm 23:4-6 (VOICE) Even in the unending shadows of death's darkness, I am not overcome by fear. Because You are with me in those dark moments, near with Your protection and guidance, I am comforted. You spread out a table before me, provisions in the midst of attack from my enemies; You care for all my needs, anointing my head with soothing, fragrant oil, filling my cup again and again with Your grace. Certainly Your faithful protection and loving provision will pursue me where I go, always, everywhere. I will always be with the Eternal, in Your house forever.*

Psalm 23:4 (TPT) Lord, even when your path takes me through the valley of deepest darkness, fear will never conquer me, for you already have! You remain close to me and lead me through it all the way. Your authority is my strength and my peace. The comfort of your love takes away my fear. I'll never be lonely, for you are near.

❊ ❊ ❊

Find Your Life in Me

John 15:4 (TLB) Take care to live in me, and let me live in you. For a branch can't produce fruit when severed from the vine. Nor can you be fruitful apart from me.

Beloved, I AM the life-giving force. Press into Me and passionately pursue My presence. In Me you find life more abundantly, contentment and peace, and refreshing for your soul. My Spirit is water in a dry and weary land, and My Word is the bread of life. Hunger and thirst and be satisfied. Find your life in Me.

Be transformed by the power of My presence. From glory unto glory, allow My Spirit to shine in and through you. May My glory reflect in your countenance as it did on Moses' face. Walk unveiled and unashamed, a living testament to your life-giving, life-changing God.

❊ ❊ ❊

Keep Your Mind Fixed on Me

> *Exodus 28:36 (KJV) And thou shalt make a plate of pure gold, and grave upon it, like the engravings of a signet, Holiness To The Lord.*

Beloved, keep your mind fixed on Me and My ways. Meditate on My word and let it so saturate who you are that your thoughts and deeds align with it without hesitation. Be so firmly rooted in My thoughts, that no suggestion that is in opposition - whether it be from human or spiritual origin - leads you astray.

Reject that which is not of Me and that which I declare evil. Refuse to give it a place in your life. For, beloved, the enemy will exploit any and every toehold he is granted, so refuse to give him access to torment you. Resist the devil and he will flee. Stand fast in truth, taking every thought captive and offering holiness unto Me.

> *2 Corinthians 10:4-5 (GW) The weapons we use in our fight are not made by humans. Rather, they are powerful weapons from God. With them we destroy people's defenses, that is, their arguments and all their intellectual arrogance that oppose the knowledge of God. We take every thought captive so that it is obedient to Christ.*

> *James 4:7 (AMP) So submit to [the authority of] God. Resist the devil [stand firm against him] and he will flee from you.*

❈ ❈ ❈

I AM the Waymaker

> *Isaiah 43:16 (TLB) I am the Lord, who opened a way through the waters, making a path right through the sea.*

Beloved, I AM the Waymaker. You need not be concerned as to how or why, just know I AM. In times of trouble, look to Me. As you do - as your faith and trust in Me is made evident in your actions and your praise - I AM lifted up. Like a standard of victory before a contending army, I AM YHVH Nissi. I AM the Lord your banner. Who can stand against Me?

I AM the Lord of the breakthrough and the restorer of your souls. I jealously guard you and love you beyond your wildest imaginings. I AM good. Refuse to be discouraged. Refuse to be impressed with the attacks that the enemy launches, refuse him the praise of acknowledgment and fix your eyes on Me, the author and finisher of your faith. Behold, I'm doing a new thing. Watch as I bring the breakthrough.

> *Isaiah 43:16-19 (VOICE) This is what the Eternal One says, the One who does the impossible, the One who makes a path through the sea, a smooth road through tumultuous waters...Don't revel only in the past, or spend all your time recounting the victories of days gone by. Watch closely: I am preparing something new; it's happening now, even as I speak, and you're about to see it. I am preparing a way through the desert; Waters will flow where there had been none.*

❊ ❊ ❊

Walk in True Liberty

> *Job 23:11 (VOICE) My foot has been securely set in His tracks; I have kept to His course of life without swerving;*

Beloved, choose not to be distressed or dismayed in the face of hardship, knowing that I AM sovereign and that I will never leave your side. I set your feet to My path and watch to steady you when you stumble. Trust that My ability to protect you is greater than your ability to mess up.

Continue to walk steadfastly along My path, knowing that My plans and purposes for you are good. Walking in alignment with Me isn't giving up your freedom, but rather walking in true liberty. So stay the course I have set you on without swerving or deviation. Trust that I AM God.

❊ ❊ ❊

Be a Radiant Reflection

> *1 John 1:1-7 (TPT) ...We testify to this truth: the eternal Life-Giver lived face-to-face with the Father and has now dawned upon us...*

Beloved, let your life and your mouth testify to the truth of who I AM. Shine before men - a radiant reflection of My glory - that those who know you might know Me. Be mindful that your words and actions align with My heart.

Do nothing to intentionally diminish the evidence of My hand in your life. There will always be those offended by Me. Remember when the world rejects you, that it first rejected Me. Walk in the truth that I have accepted you and in the end that is all that matters.

> *1 John 1:1-7 (TPT) We saw him with our very own eyes. We gazed upon him and heard him speak. Our hands actually touched him, the one who was from the beginning, the Living Expression of God. This Life-Giver was made visible and we have seen him. We testify to this truth: the eternal Life-Giver lived face-to-face with the Father and has now dawned upon us. So we proclaim to you what we have seen and heard about this Life-Giver so that we may share and enjoy this life together. For truly our fellowship is with the Father and with his Son, Jesus, the Anointed One. We are writing these things to you because we want to release to you our fullness of joy. This is the life-giving message we heard him share and it's still ringing in our ears. We now repeat his words to you: God is pure light. You will never find even a trace of darkness in him. If we claim that we share life with him, but keep walking in the realm of darkness, we're fooling ourselves and not living the truth. But if we keep living in the pure light that surrounds him, we share unbroken fellowship with one another, and the blood of Jesus, his Son, continually cleanses us from all sin.*

❊ ❊ ❊

Shine Unhindered

> *Matthew 5:43-48 (TPT) ...do something wonderful for the one who hates you...*

Beloved, refuse to let someone else's actions mandate who you are. You are My child, a reflection of Me. You operate in humility, love, truth, mercy, and integrity. None of those things are conditional on someone else's actions. Refuse to reflect someone else's poor behavior.

Refuse to indulge a fleshly desire to "be right" or "show them". Reflect love in the face of hate and humility in the face of pride, honor in the face of perversion and integrity in the face of deceit. Refuse to let anything steal your witness. Allow Me to shine through you unhindered.

> *Matthew 5:43-48 (TPT) "Your ancestors have also been taught 'Love your neighbors and hate the one who hates you.' However, I say to you, love your enemy, bless the one who curses you, do something wonderful for the one who hates you, and respond to the very ones who persecute you by praying for them. For that will reveal your identity as children of your heavenly Father. He is kind to all by bringing the sunrise to warm and rainfall to refresh whether a person does what is good or evil. What reward do you deserve if you only love the loveable? Don't even the tax collectors do that? How are you any different from others if you limit your kindness only to your friends? Don't even the ungodly do that? Since you are children of a perfect Father in heaven, you are to be perfect like him."*

❊ ❊ ❊

Look to My Spirit to Guide

> *1 Corinthians 2:16 (AMP) For who has known the mind and purposes of the Lord, so as to instruct Him? But we have the mind of Christ [to be guided by His thoughts and purposes].*

Beloved, My Spirit has been given to you to teach and guide you in all things. Nothing is too trivial for My notice, for if it concerns you, it concerns Me. So seek My face and ask My counsel. Be intentional about doing My will and living in a way that is pleasing to Me.

Refuse to be derailed by worldly compromises. Even if others' might see them as "not a big deal," know that anything that creates distance between us is significant, and not worth partaking in. Yes, beloved, I extend grace, but resist the urge to use it lightly, for it came at a high cost. Free is not valueless. It is a precious, weighty gift, so walk in righteousness, and look to My Spirit to guide.

From the Author

If you've been blessed by this book, please consider leaving a review on Amazon, Goodreads, or other places reviews are allowed. Your feedback is vital to helping others find out about Daily Downloads from Heaven. Each review matters, so thank you for considering taking the time to share!

To see the **Daily Downloads from Heaven** in action (also called *Prophetic Nuggets*), visit Dyed4youMinistries.com and find out more about our silks and artwork, which incorporate these downloads in the letters that accompany them. For a tangible reminder of your favorite download, you can purchase a prayer silk through our Etsy store (Dyed4youReadymade.com) - simply request the download by name in the note to seller as you're checking out.

If you want to share a testimony of how Papa God touched you through these daily downloads, please contact me at share@meghanw.com.

May God richly bless you as you continue to seek Him!

Cover Art Word

The Dyed4you Art piece featured on the cover is called *"Place of Rest."* A portion of the word is shared below. Several of these Prophetic Nuggets you may recognize from our Daily Downloads. The full word that goes with it can be found online in our Dyed4you Art gallery at http://dyed4youart.com/2017/02/place-of-rest/

Place of Rest brings us the sense of peace that we find in YHVH Shalom (the LORD our Peace) and that we carry from Him to the world.

> ***Psalm 132:14*** *(VOICE) This is My sanctuary, My resting place, forever and ever; I will remain here, for this is what I have desired.*

> ***Isaiah 66:1*** *(NOG) This is what Yahweh says: Heaven is my throne. The earth is my footstool. Where can you build a house or resting place for me?*

A Prophetic Nugget from Meghan Williams of Dyed4you Ministries is connected to this. It's called *"Quiet Yourself and Listen."*

> ***Psalm 27:4*** *(TPT) Here's the one thing I crave from God, the one thing I seek above all else: I want the privilege of living with him every moment in his house, finding the sweet loveliness of his face, filled with awe, delighting in his glory and grace. I want*

to live my life so close to him that he takes pleasure in my every prayer.

Beloved, in the beauty of our intimacy I cherish all you share with Me even as you are called to revere all I share with you. When you love and respect someone, you value their thoughts and dreams, requests and petitions. So I take great pleasure in yours.

There's no need to guard your heart from Me, beloved, for your heart is safe in My hands. I love you, and what matters to you, matters to Me. Can you say the same? Be sure to take the time to sit, quiet yourself, and listen. Resist the urge to rush Me to speak. Wait upon Me, and delight in My glory and grace as you gaze upon the beauty of My face.

Another Prophetic Nugget from Meghan Williams of Dyed4you Ministries is connected to this. It's called *"BE with Me."*

Beloved, step into your closet and shut the door. Take a moment to exhale and pause and just rest in Me. Inhale and receive My love, My rest, My refreshing. Resist the urge to allow yourself to be pulled so many directions that you have nothing left and are running on empty. Remember I AM your source. I AM always right here – with you and waiting – ready to fill you and refresh you. Take that moment to pause and just BE with Me. I will meet you there.

Another Prophetic Nugget from Meghan Williams of Dyed4you Ministries is connected to this. It's called *"Rest Well."*

> **Leviticus 25:4** *(NIV) But in the seventh year the land is to have a year of sabbath rest, a sabbath to the LORD. Do not sow your fields or prune your vineyards.*

Beloved, inactivity does not mean purposelessness. Rest has purpose, and it is deeply necessary. Everything I have created requires pause – room to breathe, a moment to refresh. Resist the urge to find this time wasteful.

Just as healing often takes place below the surface and out of view of the natural eye and yet its effects become known over time, so rest brings life when rightly paired with times of activity – both are essential. So be intentional with your pauses and rest well even as you labor well.

A final Prophetic Nugget from Meghan Williams of Dyed4you Ministries is connected to this. It's called *"Carry an Atmosphere of Peace."*

> **Psalm 5:3** *(AMP) In the morning, O Lord, You will hear my voice; In the morning I will prepare [a prayer and a sacrifice] for You and watch and wait [for You to speak to my heart].*

Make time to meet with Me, beloved. Come sit with Me. Wait on Me. Listen for My voice. Start your day with a pause. Allow My shalom – the peace that wars against chaos – to settle in your heart and mind. Start your day in that place of quiet, tuned into My frequency. Learn to find that place quickly and stay there.

Carry that quiet with you throughout your day. The enemy will seek to shatter it, but hold fast to it and to Me. It is your Inheritance, it belongs to you and is your right. He cannot take it away, only you can release it. So don't let go. Hold fast and walk in peace, shifting the atmosphere around you to align with that peace rather than aligning to its chaos. Find Me in that place and hold on tight, I AM with you always.

You create an atmosphere of rest. Creating a space for those who need His shalom. As you've downloaded from Him, so you share the peace of the Lord with others. You've sat before the Lord, being a place for Him to dwell – a resting place for His Spirit – and as a carrier of His presence, you bring that peace with you. That peace that wars against chaos, so as you walk into the world, you shift the atmosphere – literally bringing His peace and a sense of His rest. Be generous with what you've been given, and be mindful to guard it and not to allow the enemy to steal it from you. Rest in His peace.

Father, may we be strong in Your peace. May the rest we find in Your presence gird us up with such a strong sense of peace nothing can shake it. May we gift that peace to others by letting it flow through us, being your ambassador of peace in a world that knows much chaos.

CPSIA information can be obtained
at www.ICGtesting.com
Printed in the USA
BVHW050151190721
612153BV00001B/63